FUTURE SYSTEMS

(W)WILEY-ACADEMY

UNIQUE

BUILDING

CONTENTS

DESIGNED BY FUTURE SYSTEMS

SET BY HARDLINES LTD, CHARLBURY, OXFORD

FIRST PUBLISHED IN GREAT BRITAIN IN 2001 BY WILEY-ACADEMY

A DIVISION OF

JOHN WILEY & SONS,
BAFFINS LANE, CHICHESTER,
WEST SUSSEX. PO19 1UD

ISBN 0 471 98512 0

PRINTED AND BOUND IN ITALY

FOREWORD

It's an uncertain outcome. There are so many things that can influence the result. Weather, how the team works, how the key players perform on the day. The people back in the pavilion are always crucial. It may not be a question of winning or losing, but whether the performance remains in the memory. Things can be so different from what you expected. How the crowd reacts. What you see on the television. The commentators always wanting to predict the result before things have even started. But it is really so unpredictable, and that is, or should be, part of the charm. Sometimes it is speed which is crucial, but sometimes a clever slow delivery can bring quite different benefits. Strategy is vital, but so too are tactics – the result, for a confident team, never in doubt. You can achieve it by going on the front foot or the back, as the situation demands. Circumstance, local conditions, context, precedent – all grist to the commentator's mill. Pedigree is as important as form, style of little use without content. Success is built on solid foundations, but looks effortless. The view from the boundary is as notable in the morning as are the shadows marking the end of play. Looking back, you admire the constituent parts of what produced a great experience. In the end you admire rather than analyse. And you look for a result which is greater than the sum of its parts. Of course you are thinking about architecture, but you could just as well be thinking about cricket.

P. FINCH

CRICKET

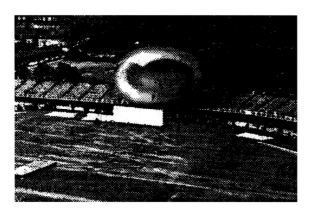

WORLD OF CRICKET

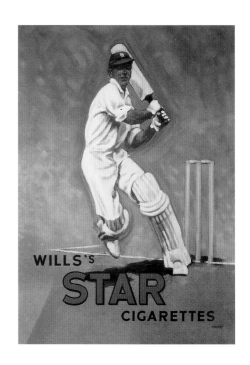

WILL'S'S
STAR
CIGARETTES

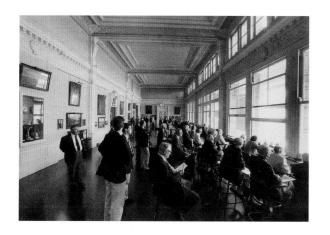

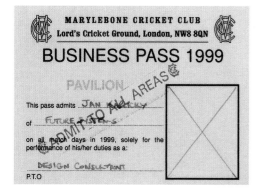

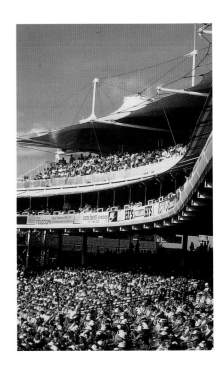

MARYLEBONE CRICKET CLUB · Lord's Cricket Ground, St. John's Wood Road, London N.W.8.

TICKET OF ADMISSION

BENSON AND HEDGES CUP

Middlesex v. Hampshire

Sunday, 23rd April 1995

COMPLIMENTARY

No. 0135

£6

No. 0135

THIS TICKET IS FOR ADMISSION FOR THE ABOVE MATCH ONLY AND IS NOT VALID ON THE FIRST DAY
UNLESS PRESENTED AT THE GATE WITH BOTH PORTIONS INTACT.
Play is not guaranteed and in no circumstances can any money be refunded.

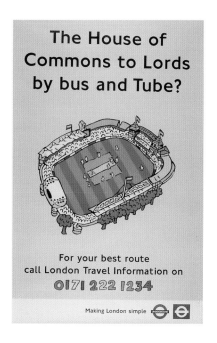

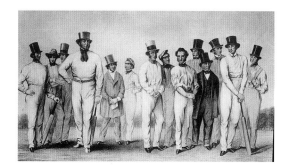

"There didn't seem much point in carrying on!"

9

1990

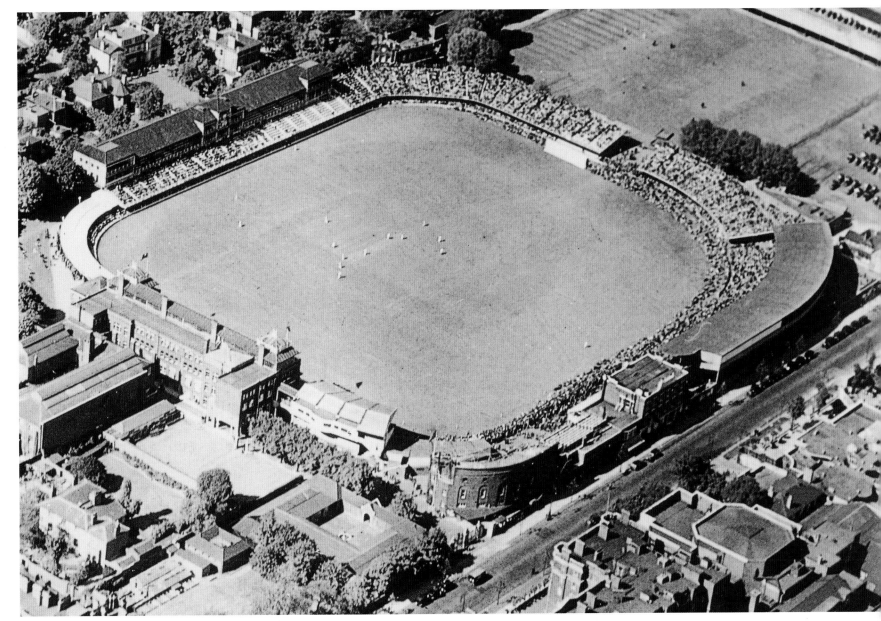

1939 PHOTO© AEROFILMS

INSPIRATION

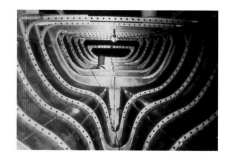

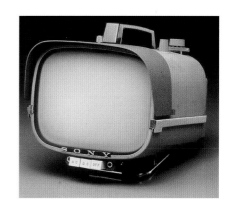

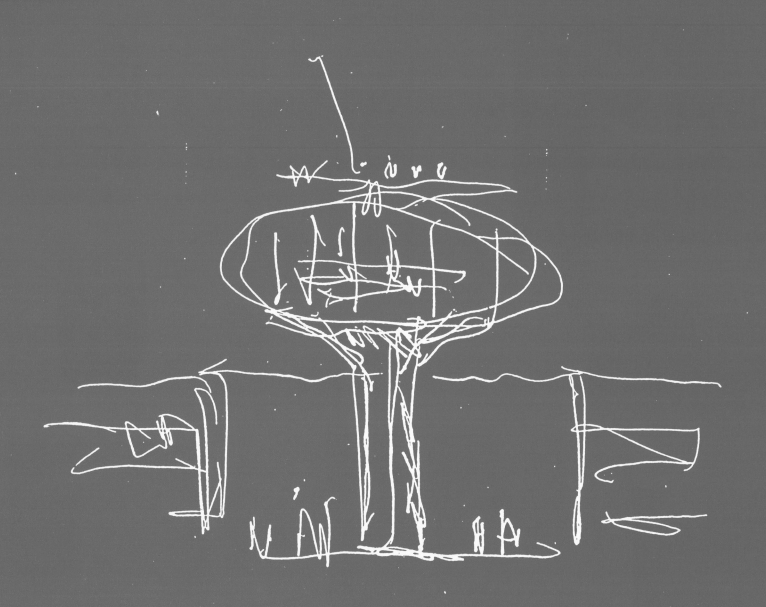

FIRST SKETCH FLIGHT LONDON–PRAGUE   19–1–95

STAIR1

STAIR

BOX

BOT

1995–1996

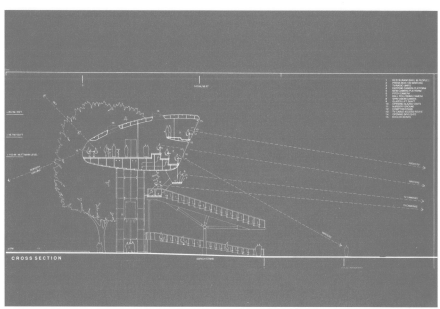

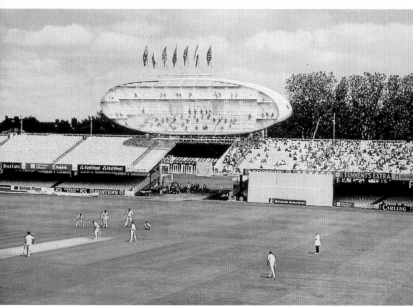

1995

1995

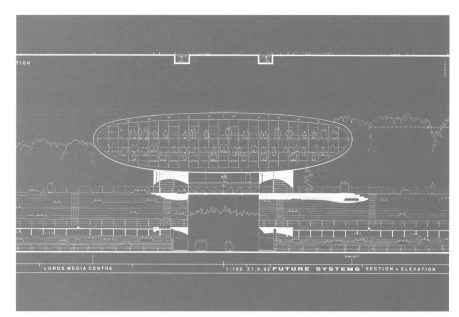

LORDS MEDIA CENTRE 1:100 21.9.95 FUTURE SYSTEMS SECTION + ELEVATION

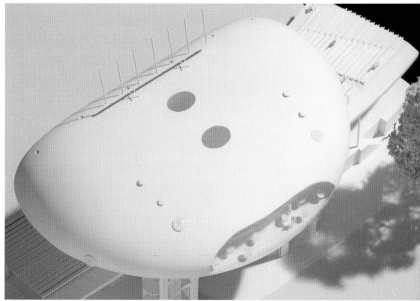

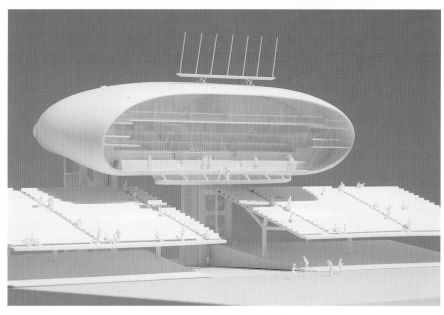

1995

1995

1 9 9 6 ⇨

SEPT 96

FEB 97

SEPT 1996 - FEB 1997

FOUNDATIONS

TOWERS

MANUFACTURING

⇨

FEB - MAR 1997

1 9 9 7

MARCH - APRIL 1997

TRANSPORT

ASSEMBLY

FITTING OUT & LIFTS

BUILDING SEQUENCE

MEDIA CENTRE

VIEW TO BOUNDARY

BOUNDARY 12M

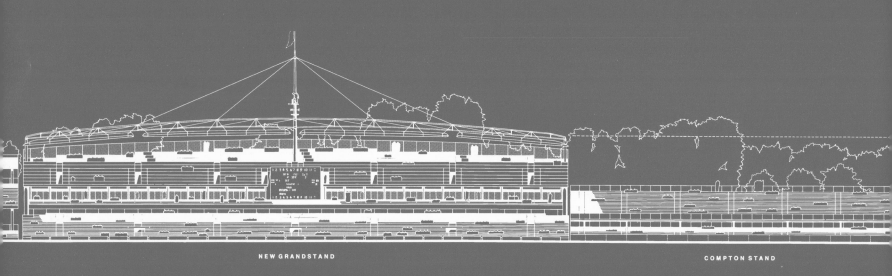

NEW GRANDSTAND

COMPTON STAND

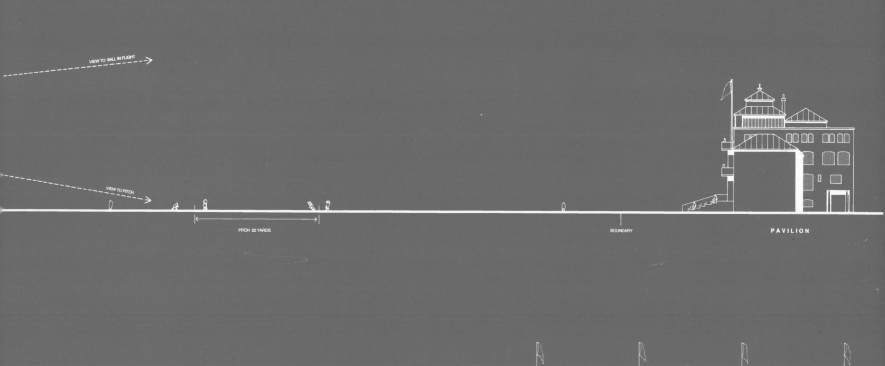

VIEW TO BALL IN FLIGHT →

VIEW TO PITCH →

PITCH 22 YARDS

BOUNDARY

PAVILION

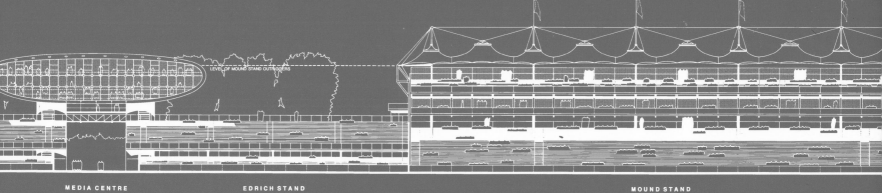

LEVEL OF MOUND STAND OUTRIGGERS

MEDIA CENTRE

EDRICH STAND

MOUND STAND

1995 COMPETITION DRAWINGS

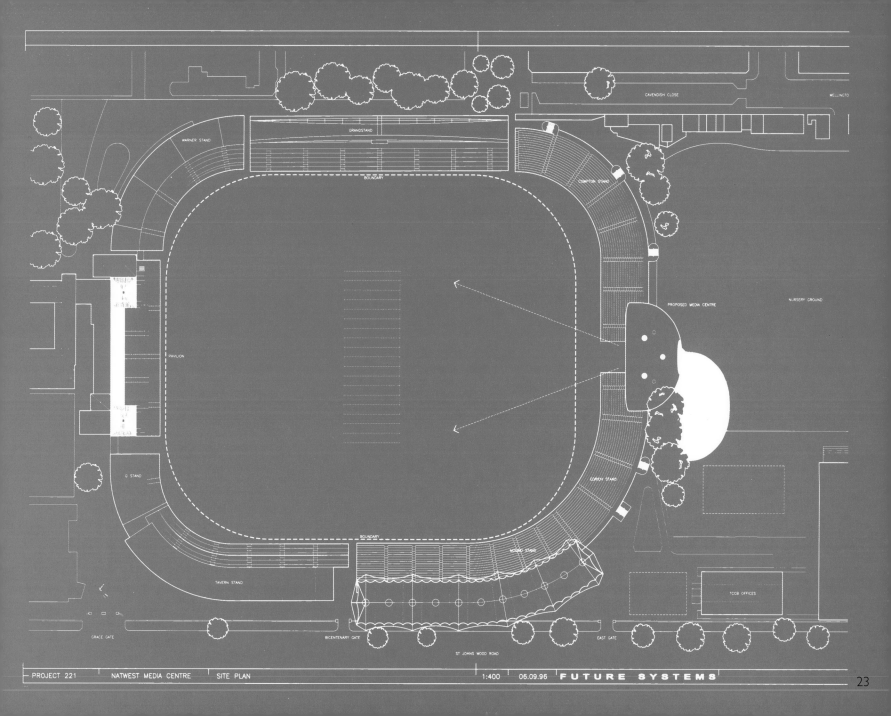

CAVENDISH CLOSE

WELLINGTO

WARNER STAND

GRANDSTAND

COMPTON STAND

BOUNDARY

PROPOSED MEDIA CENTRE

NURSERY GROUND

PAVILION

G STAND

EDRICH STAND

BOUNDARY

MOUND STAND

TAVERN STAND

TCCB OFFICES

GRACE GATE

BICENTENARY GATE

EAST GATE

ST JOHNS WOOD ROAD

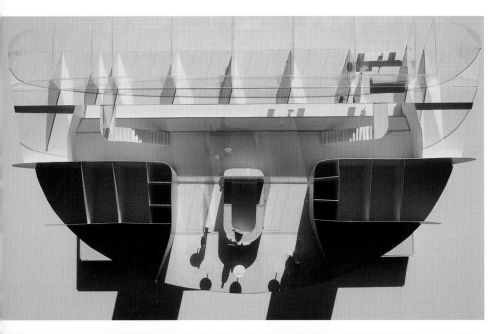

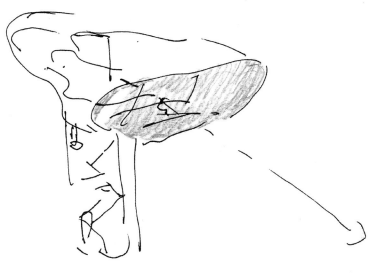

1996

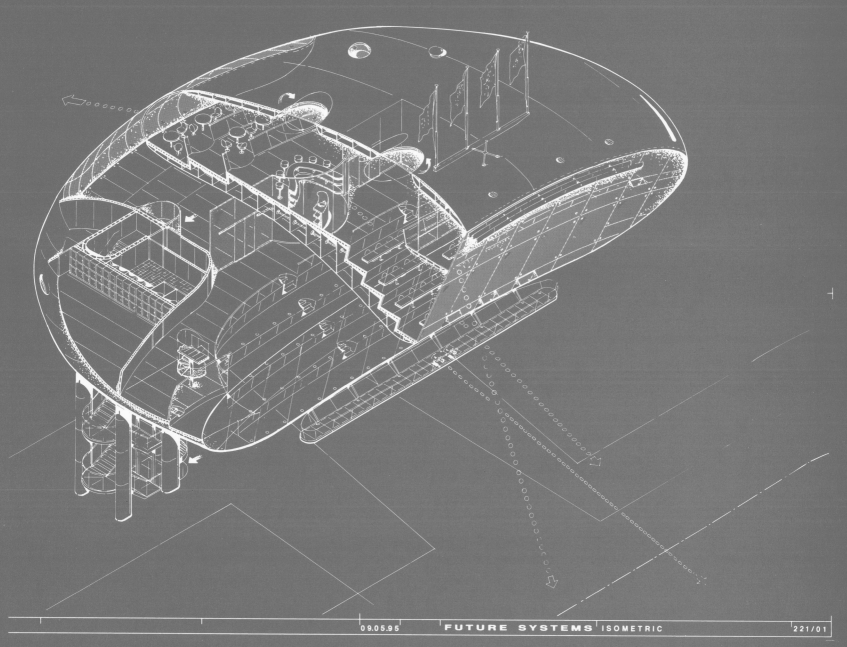

09.05.95   **FUTURE SYSTEMS** ISOMETRIC   221/01

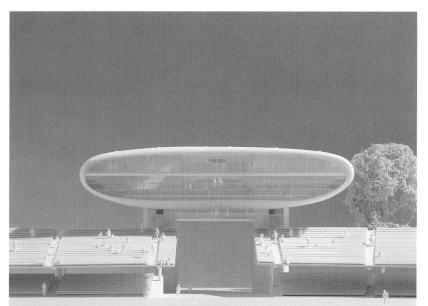

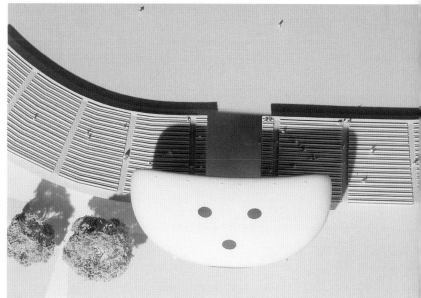

1996

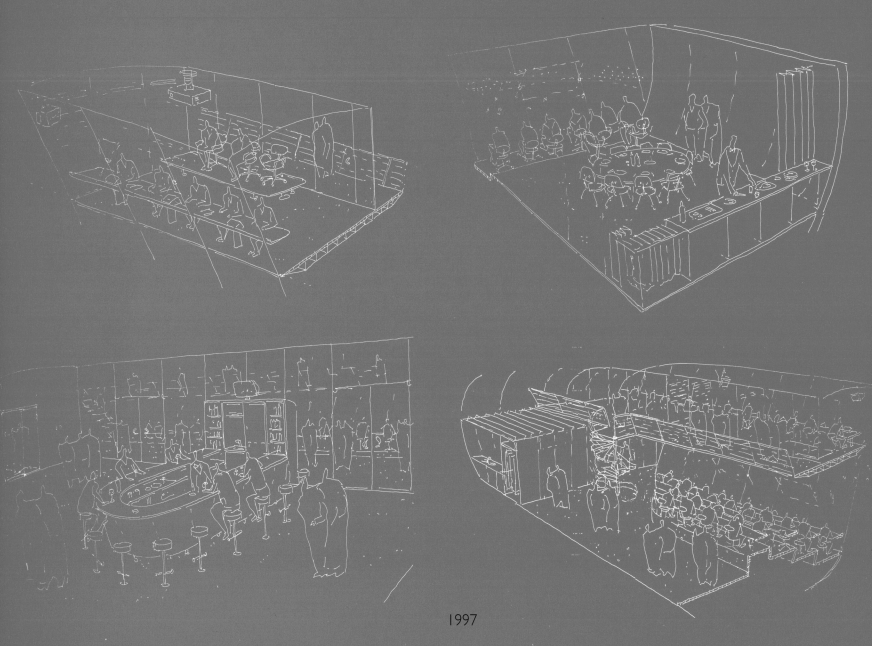

1997

RESTAURANT BAR

1997

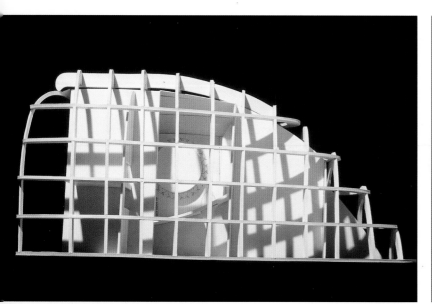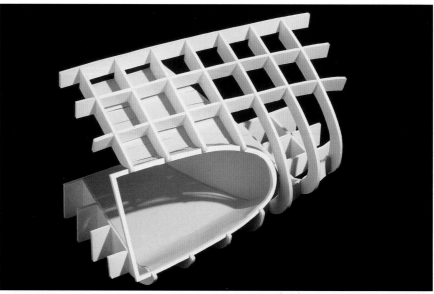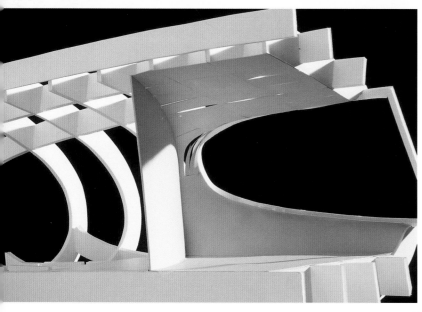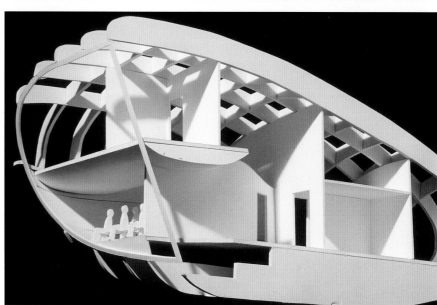

1997

1997

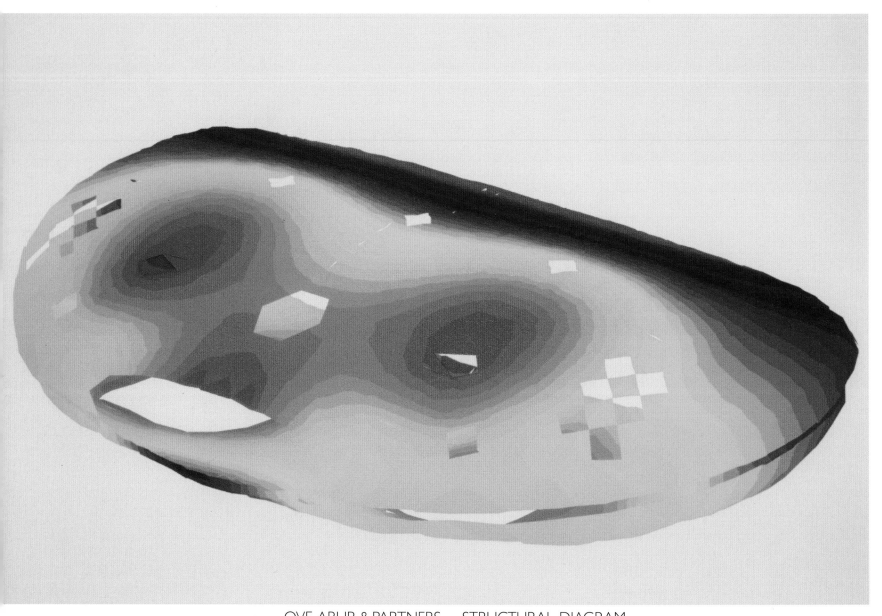

OVE ARUP & PARTNERS – STRUCTURAL DIAGRAM

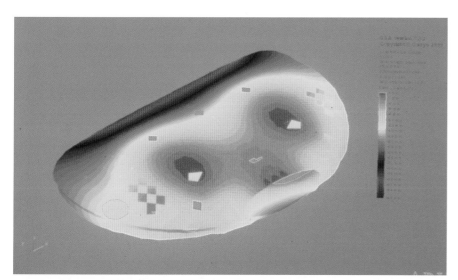

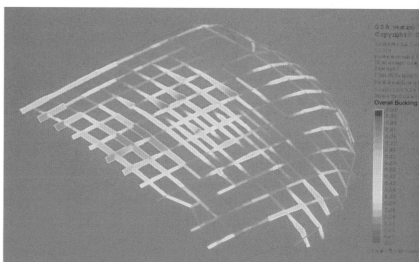

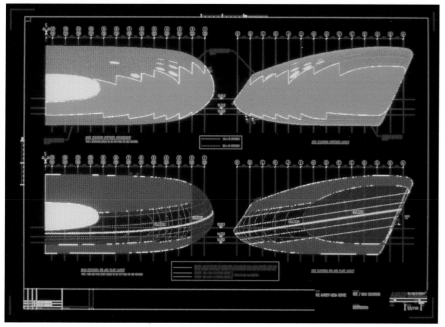

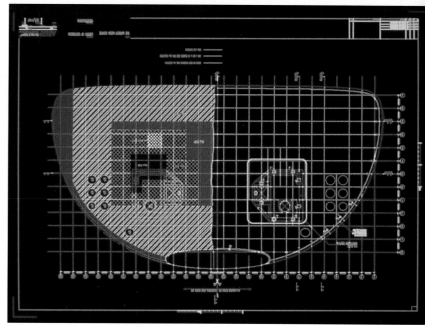

OVE ARUP & PARTNERS – STRUCTURAL DIAGRAMS

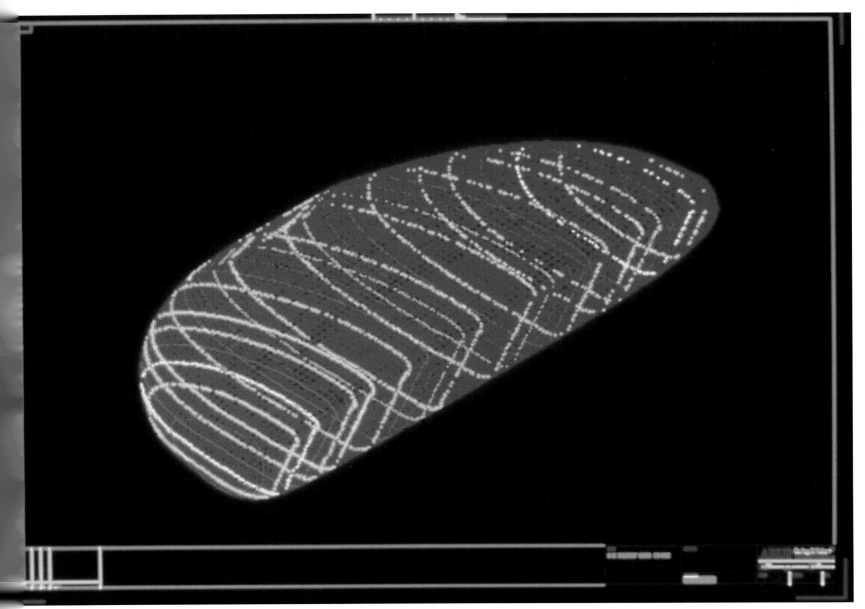

OVE ARUP & PARTNERS – FORM FINDING

1997 – FUTURE SYSTEMS FORM FINDING

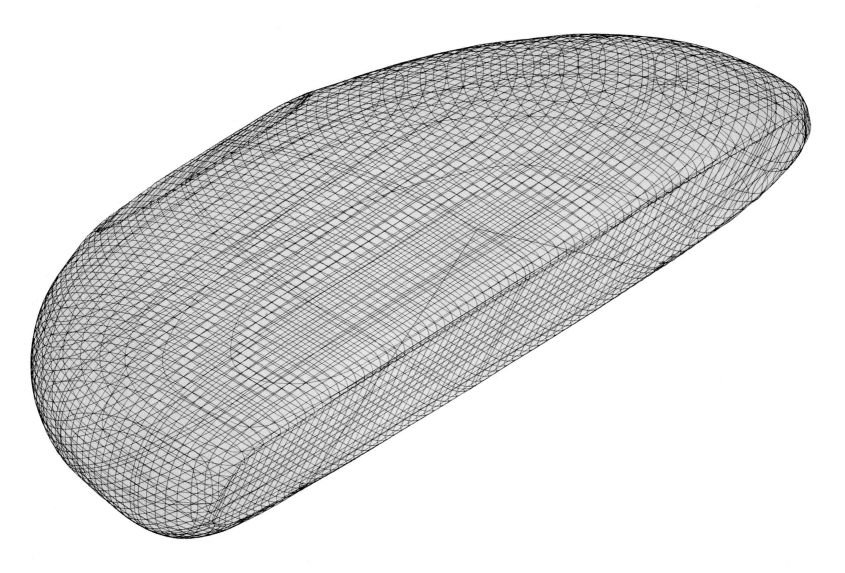

FUTURE SYSTEMS FORM FINDING

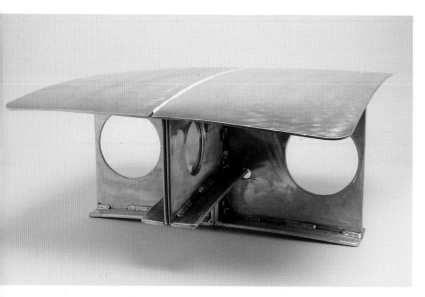

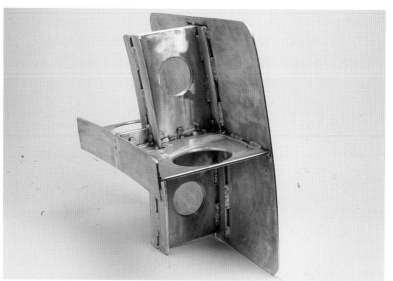

ELEMENTS – TRANSPORTATION

ARTIFICIAL SKY

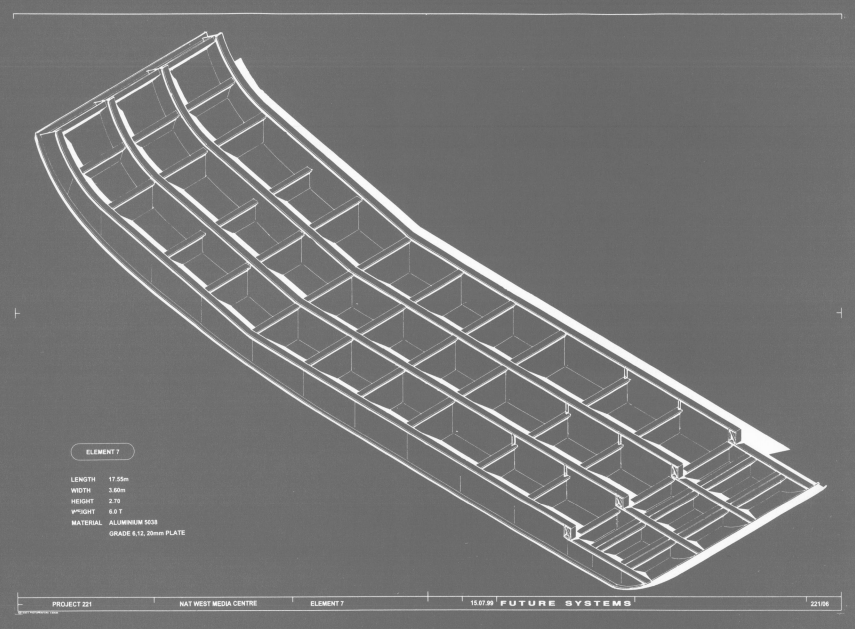

ELEMENT 7

LENGTH   17.55m
WIDTH   3.60m
HEIGHT   2.70
WEIGHT   6.0 T
MATERIAL   ALUMINIUM 5038
            GRADE 6,12, 20mm PLATE

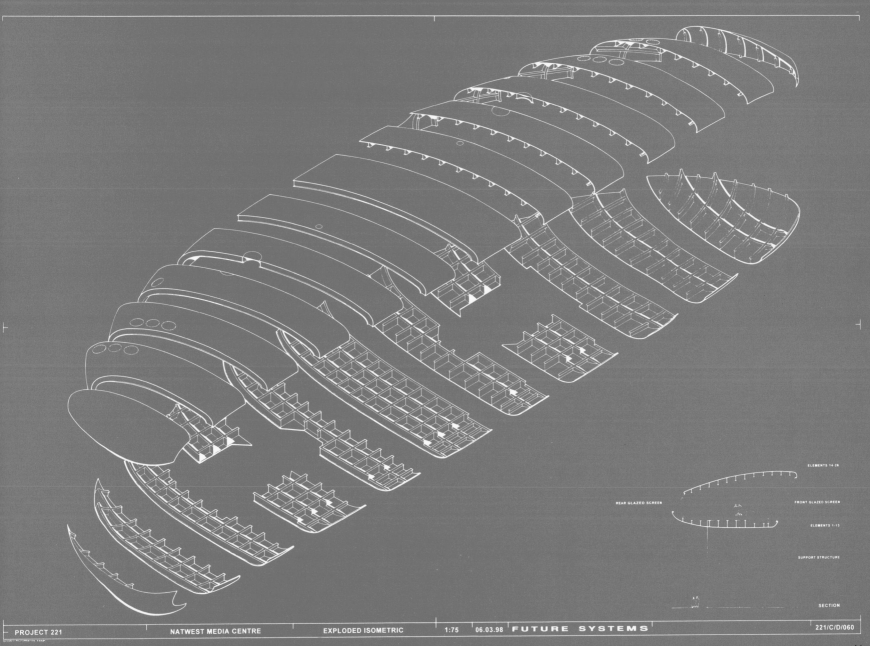

ELEMENTS 14-26

REAR GLAZED SCREEN   FRONT GLAZED SCREEN

ELEMENTS 1-13

SUPPORT STRUCTURE

SECTION

PROJECT 221   NATWEST MEDIA CENTRE   EXPLODED ISOMETRIC   1:75   06.03.98   FUTURE SYSTEMS   221/C/D/060

41

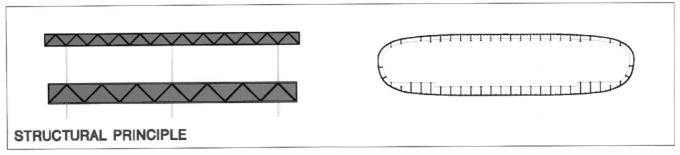

STRUCTURAL PRINCIPLE

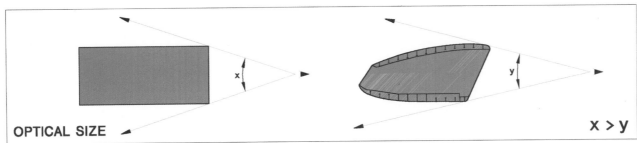

OPTICAL SIZE

x

y

x > y

1998

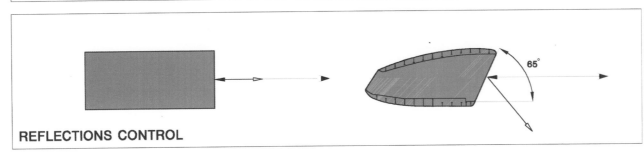

REFLECTIONS CONTROL

65°

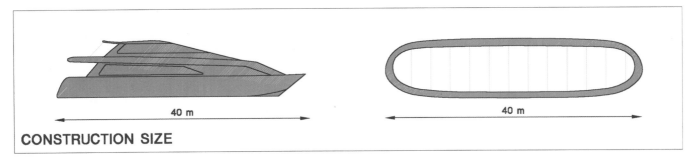

40 m

40 m

CONSTRUCTION SIZE

42

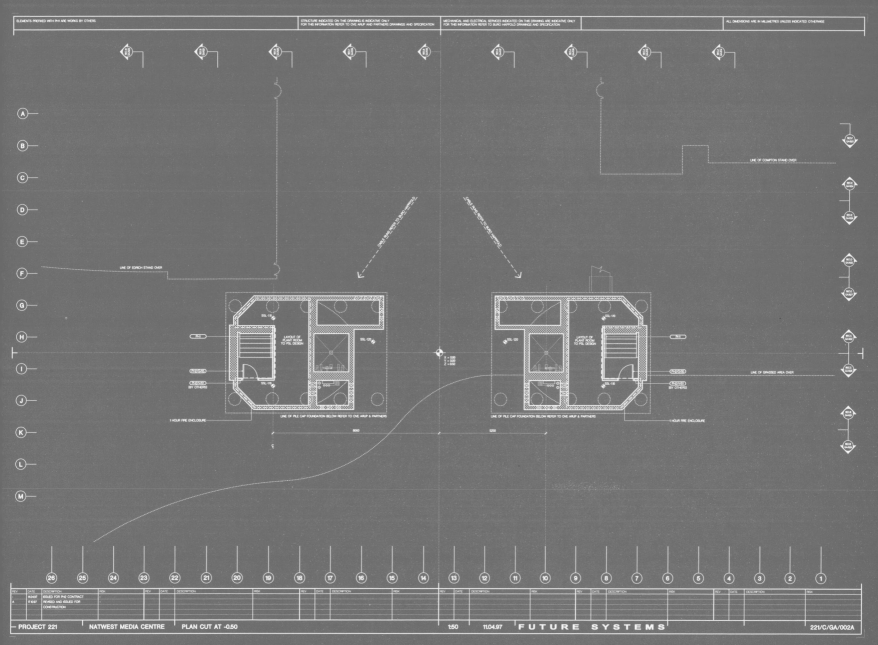

ELEMENTS PREFIXED WITH PH1 ARE WORKS BY OTHERS

STRUCTURE INDICATED ON THIS DRAWING IS INDICATIVE ONLY
FOR THIS INFORMATION REFER TO OVE ARUP AND PARTNERS DRAWINGS AND SPECIFICATION

MECHANICAL AND ELECTRICAL SERVICES INDICATED ON THIS DRAWING ARE INDICATIVE ONLY
FOR THIS INFORMATION REFER TO BURO HAPPOLD DRAWINGS AND SPECIFICATION

ALL DIMENSIONS ARE IN MILLIMETRES UNLESS INDICATED OTHERWISE

LINE OF COMPTON STAND OVER

LINE OF EDRICH STAND OVER

LAYOUT OF
PLANT ROOM
TO PSL DESIGN

LAYOUT OF
PLANT ROOM
TO PSL DESIGN

LINE OF GRASSED AREA OVER

1 HOUR FIRE ENCLOSURE

LINE OF PILE CAP FOUNDATION BELOW REFER TO OVE ARUP & PARTNERS

LINE OF PILE CAP FOUNDATION BELOW REFER TO OVE ARUP & PARTNERS

1 HOUR FIRE ENCLOSURE

PROVIDED
BY OTHERS

PROVIDED
BY OTHERS

PROJECT 221   NATWEST MEDIA CENTRE   PLAN CUT AT -0.50

1:50   11.04.97   F U T U R E   S Y S T E M S   221/C/GA/002A

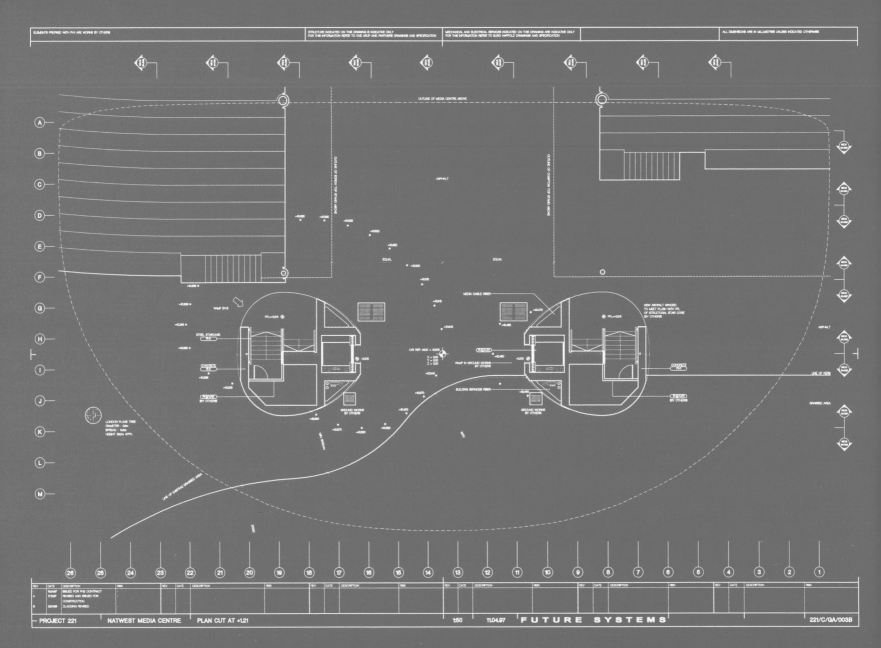

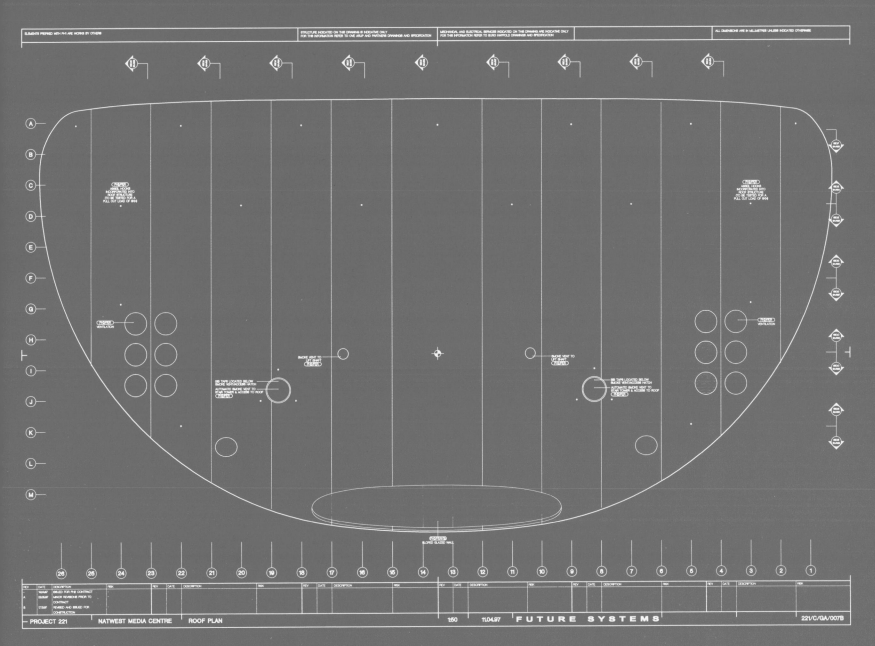

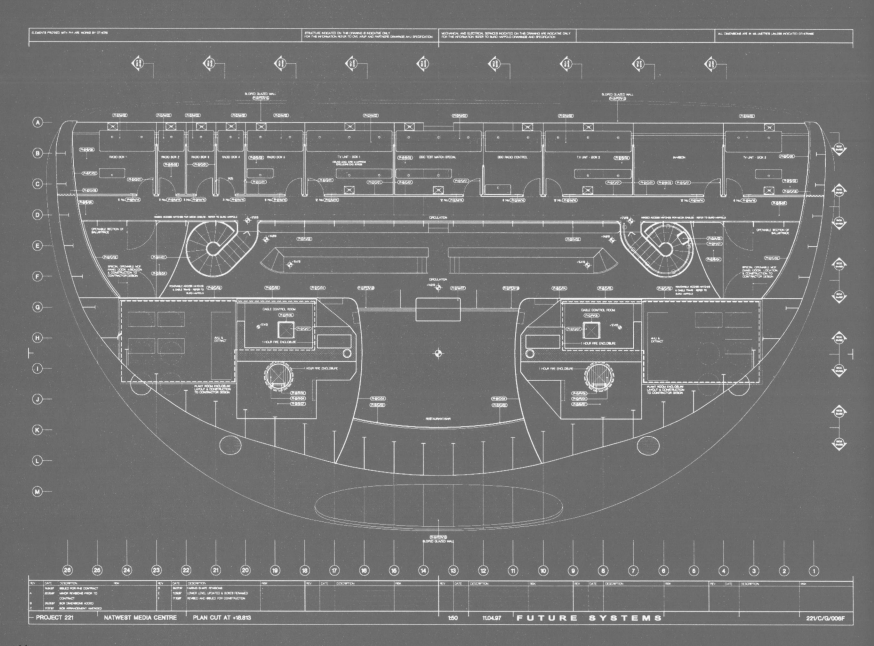

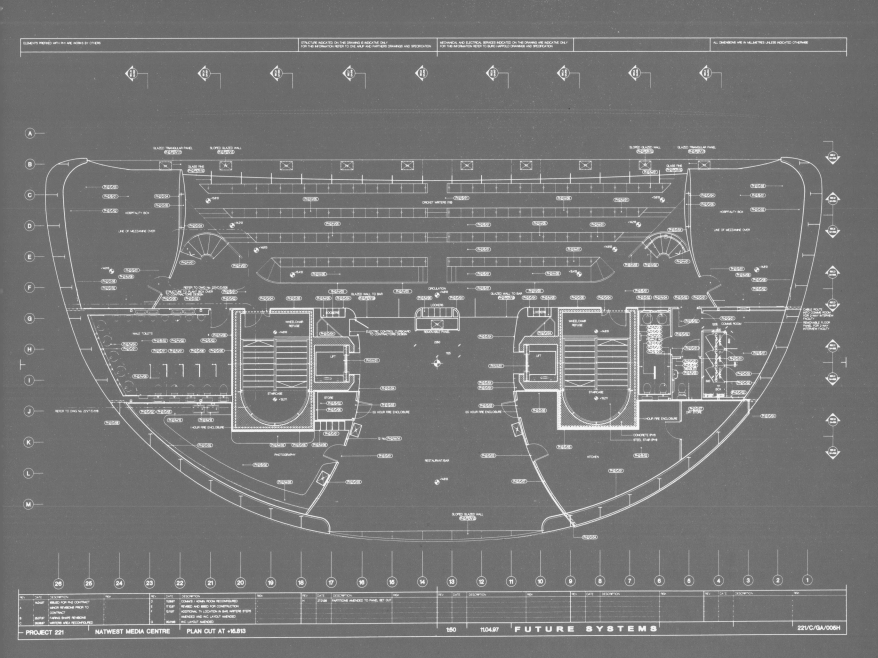

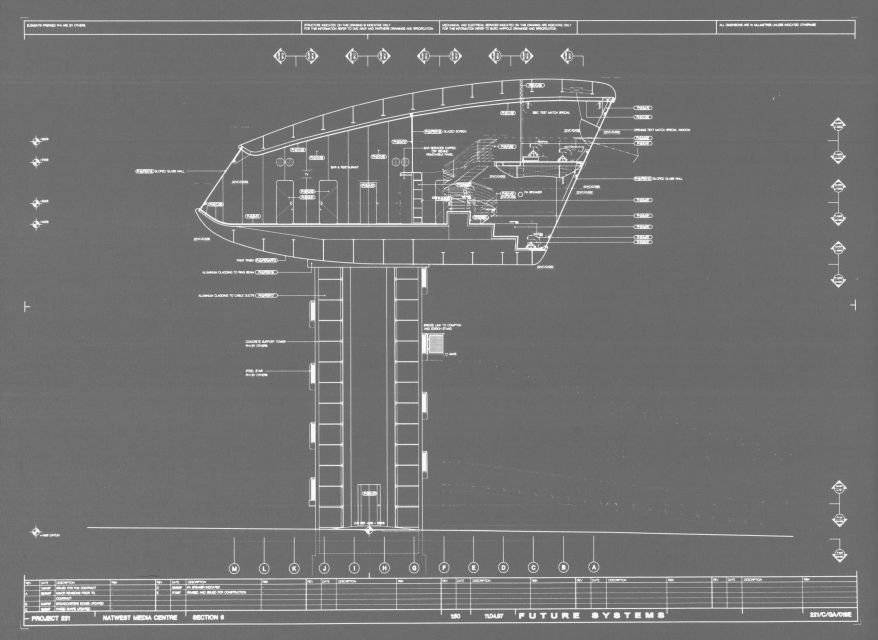

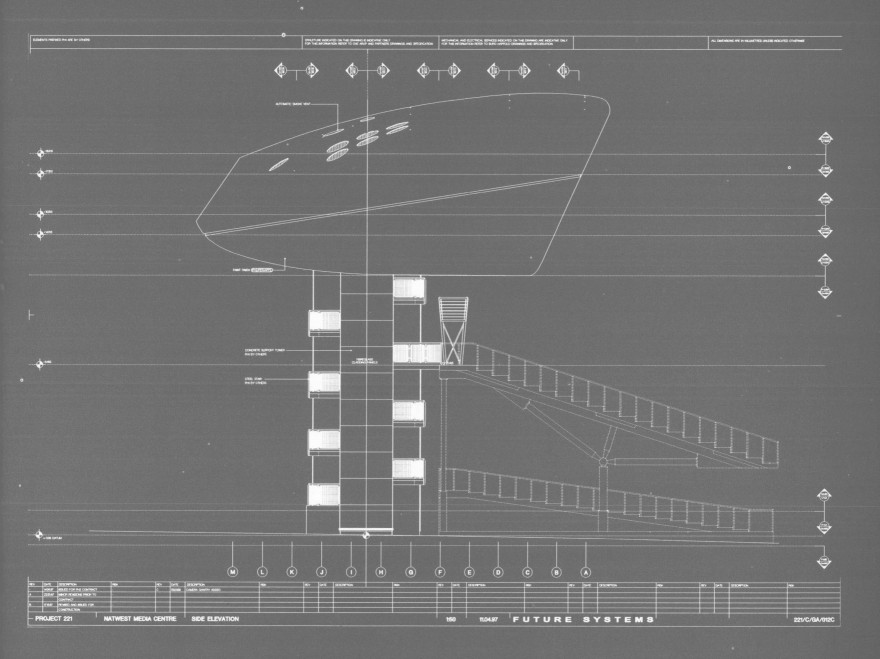

PROJECT 221   NATWEST MEDIA CENTRE   SIDE ELEVATION   1:50   11.04.97   F U T U R E   S Y S T E M S   221/C/GA/012C

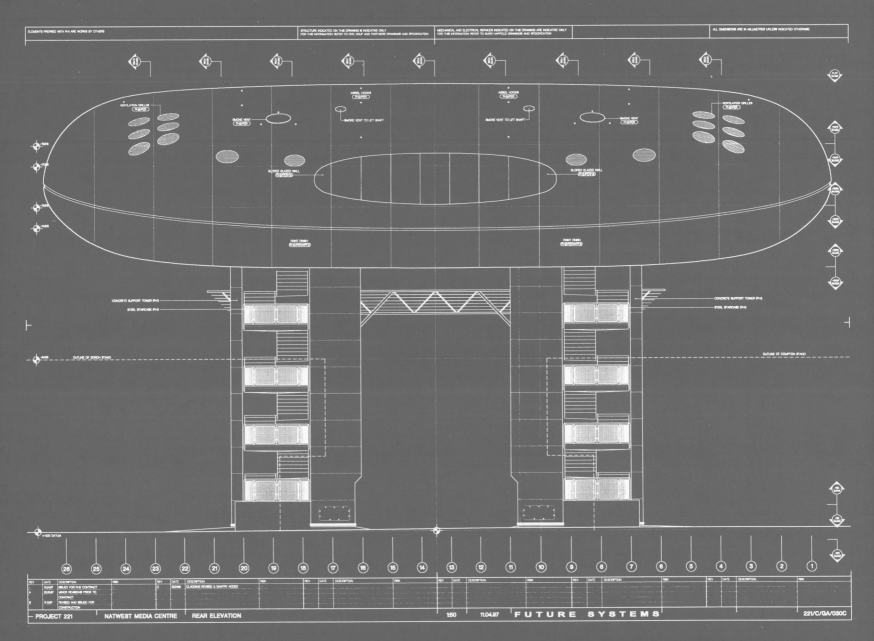

PROJECT 221   NATWEST MEDIA CENTRE   REAR ELEVATION   1:50   11.04.97   FUTURE SYSTEMS   221/C/GA/030C

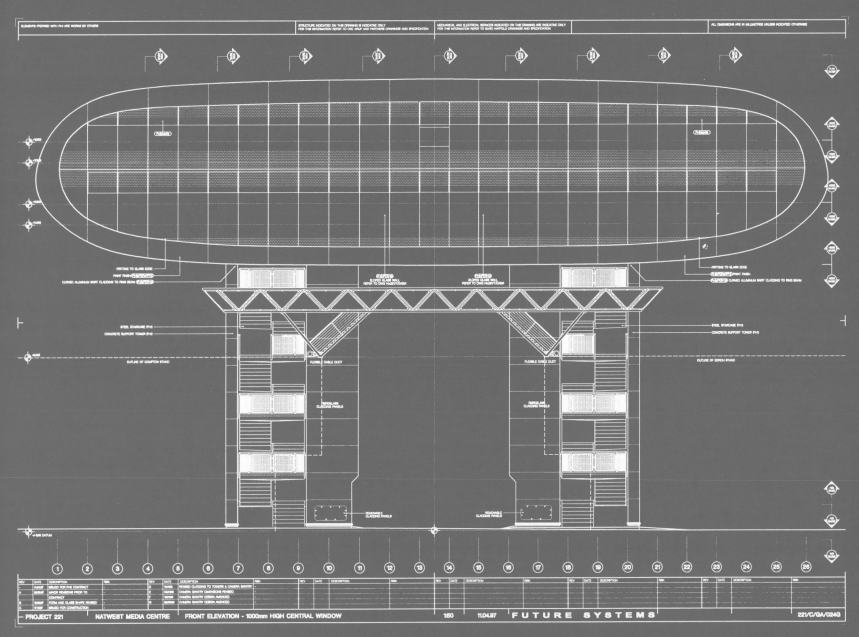

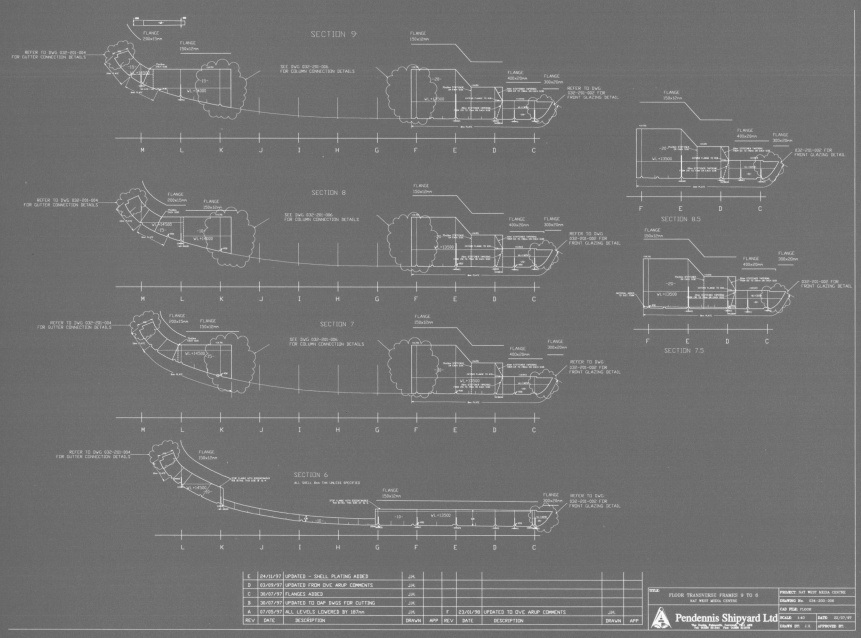

SECTION 9

SECTION 8

SECTION 8.5

SECTION 7

SECTION 7.5

SECTION 6
ALL SHELL 8mm THK UNLESS SPECIFIED

REV	DATE	DESCRIPTION	DRAWN	APP	REV	DATE	DESCRIPTION	DRAWN	APP
E	24/11/97	UPDATED - SHELL PLATING ADDED	J.H.						
D	03/09/97	UPDATED FROM OVE ARUP COMMENTS	J.H.						
C	30/07/97	FLANGES ADDED	J.H.						
B	30/07/97	UPDATED TO DAP DWGS FOR CUTTING	J.H.						
A	07/05/97	ALL LEVELS LOWERED BY 187mm	J.H.		F	23/01/98	UPDATED TO OVE ARUP COMMENTS	J.H.	

Pendennis Shipyard Ltd
The Docks, Falmouth, Cornwall, TR11 4NR
Tel: 01326 211344 Fax: 01326 211679

TITLE: FLOOR TRANSVERSE FRAMES 9 TO 6
NAT WEST MEDIA CENTRE

PROJECT: NAT WEST MEDIA CENTRE
DRAWING No.: 034-200-006
CAD FILE: FLOOR
SCALE: 1:40   DATE: 22/07/97
DRAWN BY: J.H.   APPROVED BY:

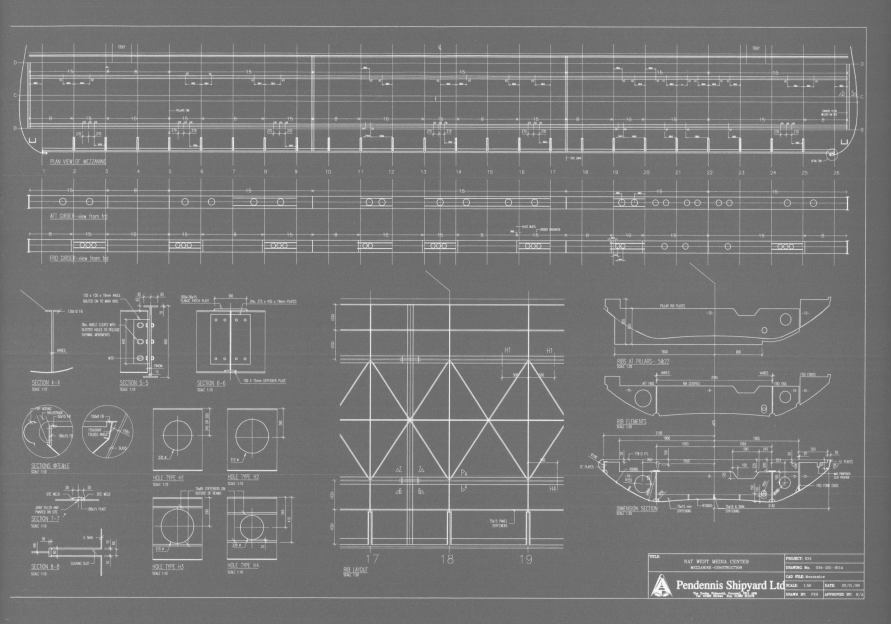

PLAN VIEW OF MEZZANINE

AFT GIRDER—view from frd

FRD GIRDER—view from frd

SECTION 4-4
SCALE 1:10

SECTION 5-5
SCALE 1:10

SECTION 6-6
SCALE 1:10

SECTIONS @TE&LE
SCALE 1:10

SECTION 7-7
SCALE 1:10

SECTION 8-8
SCALE 1:10

HOLE TYPE H1
SCALE 1:10

HOLE TYPE H2
SCALE 1:10

HOLE TYPE H3
SCALE 1:10

HOLE TYPE H4
SCALE 1:10

RIB LAYOUT
SCALE 1:30

RIBS AT PILLARS— 5&22
SCALE 1:20

RIB ELEMENTS
SCALE 1:30

DIMENSION SECTION
SCALE 1:30

TITLE:
NAT WEST MEDIA CENTER
MEZZANINE—CONSTRUCTION

Pendennis Shipyard Ltd
The Docks, Falmouth, Cornwall, TR11 4NR
Tel: 01326 211344 Fax: 01326 211079

PROJECT: 034
DRAWING No. 034-201-011A
CAD FILE: Mezzanine
SCALE: 1:50   DATE: 20/01/99
DRAWN BY: PJB   APPROVED BY: N/A

53

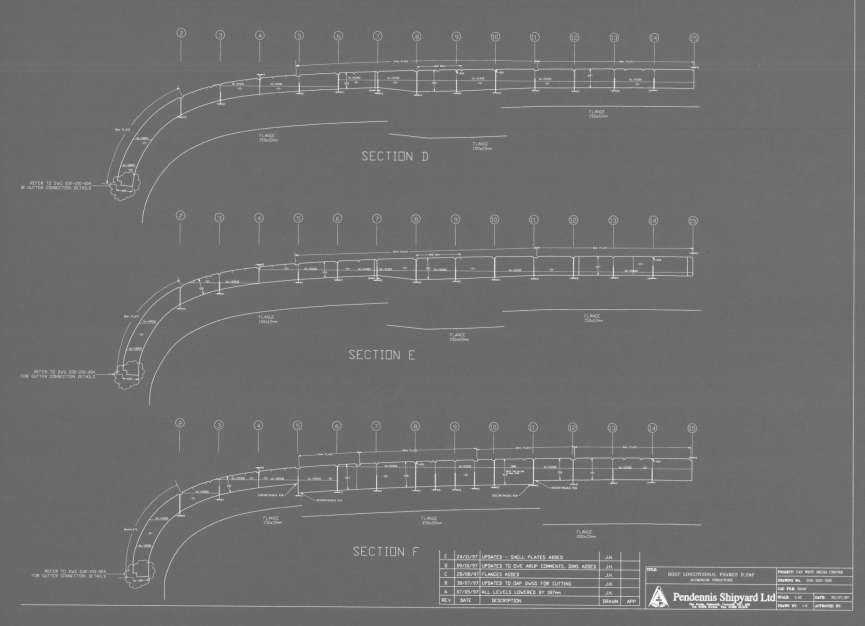

SECTION D

SECTION E

SECTION F

REFER TO DWG 032-201-004
FOR GUTTER CONNECTION DETAILS

REFER TO DWG 032-201-004
FOR GUTTER CONNECTION DETAILS

REFER TO DWG 032-201-004
FOR GUTTER CONNECTION DETAILS

FLANGE
150x12mm

FLANGE
350x20mm

FLANGE
200x15mm

REV	DATE	DESCRIPTION	DRAWN	APP
E	24/11/97	UPDATED - SHELL PLATES ADDED	J.H.	
D	09/10/97	UPDATED TO OVE ARUP COMMENTS, DIMS ADDED	J.H.	
C	28/08/97	FLANGES ADDED	J.H.	
B	30/07/97	UPDATED TO OAP DWGS FOR CUTTING	J.H.	
A	07/05/97	ALL LEVELS LOWERED BY 187mm	J.H.	

TITLE:
ROOF LONGITUDINAL FRAMES D,E&F
ALUMINIUM STRUCTURE

Pendennis Shipyard Ltd

PROJECT: NAT WEST MEDIA CENTRE

DRAWING No.   034-200-009

CAD FILE: ROOF

SCALE: 1:40   DATE: 30/07/97

DRAWN BY: J.H.   APPROVED BY:

54

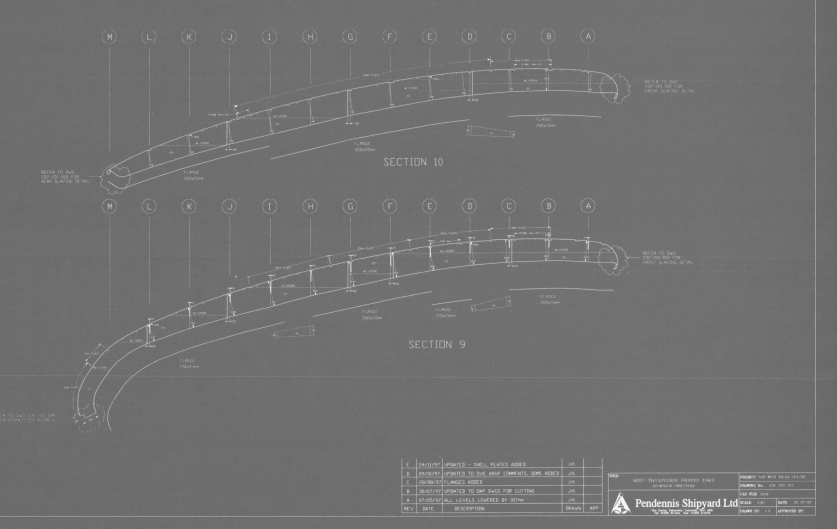

SECTION 10

SECTION 9

REFER TO DWG
032-201-003 FOR
REAR GLAZING DETAIL

REFER TO DWG
032-201-002 FOR
FRONT GLAZING DETAIL

REFER TO DWG
032-201-002 FOR
FRONT GLAZING DETAIL

E	24/11/97	UPDATED - SHELL PLATES ADDED	J.H.	
D	09/10/97	UPDATED TO OVE ARUP COMMENTS, DIMS ADDED	J.H.	
C	28/08/97	FLANGES ADDED	J.H.	
B	30/07/97	UPDATED TO DAP DWGS FOR CUTTING	J.H.	
A	07/05/97	ALL LEVELS LOWERED BY 187mm	J.H.	
REV	DATE	DESCRIPTION	DRAWN	APP

TITLE
ROOF TRANSVERSE FRAMES 10&9
ALUMINIUM STRUCTURE

Pendennis Shipyard Ltd
The Docks, Falmouth, Cornwall TR11 4NR
Tel. 01326 211344 Fax. 01326 211679

PROJECT: NAT WEST MEDIA CENTRE
DRAWING No. 032-200-013
CAD FILE: XXXX
SCALE: 1:40   DATE: 30.07.97
DRAWN BY: J.H.   APPROVED BY:

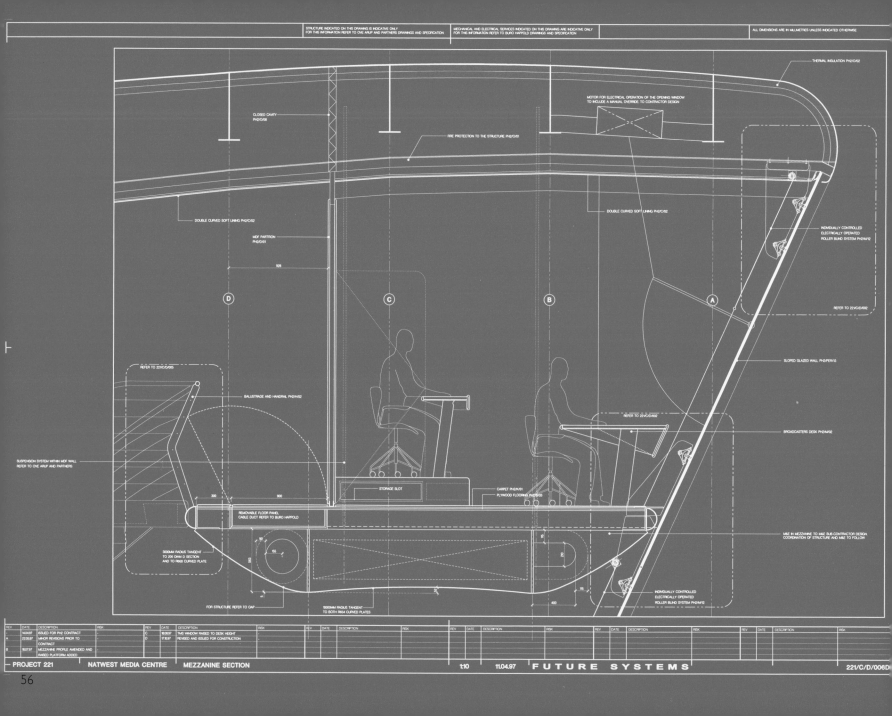

STRUCTURE INDICATED ON THIS DRAWING IS INDICATIVE ONLY
FOR THIS INFORMATION REFER TO OVE ARUP AND PARTNERS DRAWINGS AND SPECIFICATION

MECHANICAL AND ELECTRICAL SERVICES INDICATED ON THIS DRAWING ARE INDICATIVE ONLY
FOR THIS INFORMATION REFER TO BURO HAPPOLD DRAWINGS AND SPECIFICATION

ALL DIMENSIONS ARE IN MILLIMETRES UNLESS INDICATED OTHERWISE

THERMAL INSULATION PH2/C/52

MOTOR FOR ELECTRICAL OPERATION OF THE OPENING WINDOW
TO INCLUDE A MANUAL OVERRIDE. TO CONTRACTOR DESIGN

CLOSED CAVITY
PH2/C/58

FIRE PROTECTION TO THE STRUCTURE PH2/C/51

DOUBLE CURVED SOFT LINING PH2/C/52

DOUBLE CURVED SOFT LINING PH2/C/52

INDIVIDUALLY CONTROLLED
ELECTRICALLY OPERATED
ROLLER BLIND SYSTEM PH2/M/12

MDF PARTITION
PH2/D/01

928

REFER TO 221/C/D/002

D   C   B   A

SLOPED GLAZED WALL PH2/PER/15

REFER TO 221/C/D/005

BALUSTRADE AND HANDRAIL PH2/H/02

BROADCASTERS DESK PH2/M/02

SUSPENSION SYSTEM WITHIN MDF WALL
REFER TO OVE ARUP AND PARTNERS

REFER TO 221/C/D/002

CARPET PH2/M/01
PLYWOOD FLOORING PH2/S/03

STORAGE SLOT

300   900

REMOVABLE FLOOR PANEL
CABLE DUCT REFER TO BURO HAPPOLD

M&E IN MEZZANINE TO M&E SUB-CONTRACTOR DESIGN.
COORDINATION OF STRUCTURE AND M&E TO FOLLOW

3000MM RADIUS TANGENT
TO 200 DIAM D SECTION
AND TO R658 CURVED PLATE

INDIVIDUALLY CONTROLLED
ELECTRICALLY OPERATED
ROLLER BLIND SYSTEM PH2/M/12

FOR STRUCTURE REFER TO OAP

10000MM RADIUS TANGENT
TO BOTH R654 CURVED PLATES

400

REV	DATE	DESCRIPTION	RISK	REV	DATE	DESCRIPTION	RISK	REV	DATE	DESCRIPTION	RISK	REV	DATE	DESCRIPTION	RISK	REV	DATE	DESCRIPTION	RISK	REV	DATE	DESCRIPTION	RISK
	14.04.97	ISSUED FOR PH2 CONTRACT		C	18.06.97	THIS WINDOW RAISED TO DESK HEIGHT																	
A	22.05.97	MINOR REVISIONS PRIOR TO		D	17.10.97	REVISED AND ISSUED FOR CONSTRUCTION																	
		CONTRACT																					
B	18.07.97	MEZZANINE PROFILE AMENDED AND																					
		RAISED PLATFORM ADDED																					

PROJECT 221   NATWEST MEDIA CENTRE   MEZZANINE SECTION   1:10   11.04.97   FUTURE SYSTEMS   221/C/D/006D

56

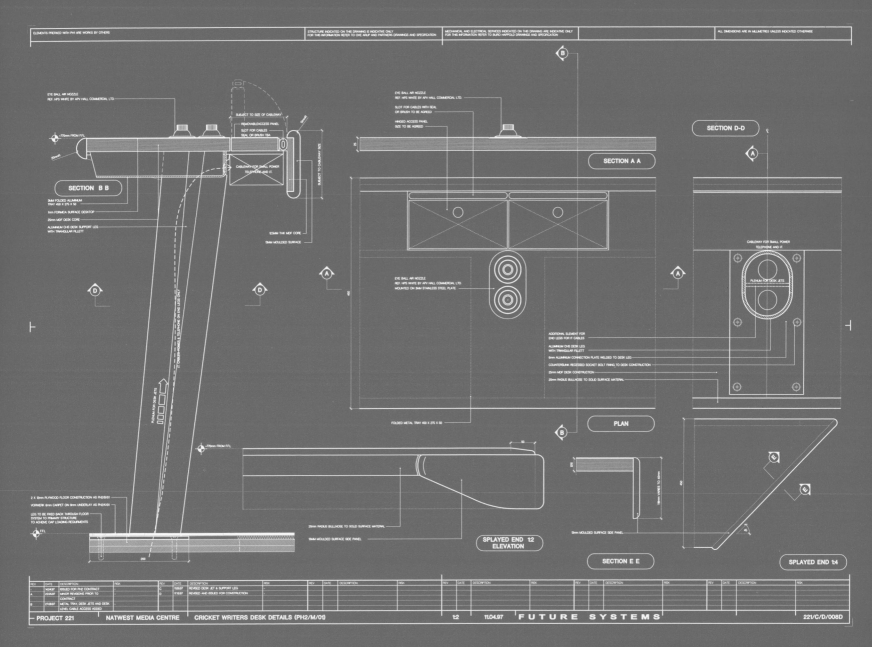

SECTION B B

EYE BALL AIR NOZZLE
REF. HPS WHITE BY APV HALL COMMERCIAL LTD.

SUBJECT TO SIZE OF CABLEWAY

REMOVABLE ACCESS PANEL

SLOT FOR CABLES
SEAL OR BRUSH TBA

CABLEWAY FOR SMALL POWER
TELEPHONE AND I.T.

~770mm FROM F.F.L.

25mm

3MM FOLDED ALUMINIUM
TRAY 450 X 275 X 50

1mm FORMICA SURFACE DESKTOP

25mm MDF DESK CORE

ALUMINIUM CHS DESK SUPPORT LEG
WITH TRIANGULAR FILLETT

125mm THK MDF CORE

3MM MOULDED SURFACE

I.T. CABLES CABLE & TELEPHONE ON END LEGS ONLY

PLENUM FOR DESK JETS

2 X 18mm PLYWOOD FLOOR CONSTRUCTION AS PH2/8/01

VORWERK 6mm CARPET ON 9mm UNDERLAY AS PH2/0/01

LEGS TO BE FIXED BACK THROUGH FLOOR
SYSTEM TO PRIMARY STRUCTURE
TO ACHIEVE CAP LOADING REQUIREMENTS

F.F.L.

200

SECTION A A

EYE BALL AIR NOZZLE
REF. HPS WHITE BY APV HALL COMMERCIAL LTD.

SLOT FOR CABLES WITH SEAL
OR BRUSH TO BE AGREED

HINGED ACCESS PANEL
SIZE TO BE AGREED

EYE BALL AIR NOZZLE
REF. HPS WHITE BY APV HALL COMMERCIAL LTD.
MOUNTED ON 3MM STAINLESS STEEL PLATE

ADDITIONAL ELEMENT FOR
END LEGS FOR I.T. CABLES

ALUMINIUM CHS DESK LEG
WITH TRIANGULAR FILLETT

6mm ALUMINIUM CONNECTION PLATE WELDED TO DESK LEG

COUNTERSUNK RECESSED SOCKET BOLT FIXING TO DESK CONSTRUCTION

25mm MDF DESK CONSTRUCTION

20mm RADIUS BULLNOSE TO SOLID SURFACE MATERIAL

FOLDED METAL TRAY 450 X 275 X 50

PLAN

SECTION D-D

CABLEWAY FOR SMALL POWER
TELEPHONE AND I.T.

PLENUM FOR DESK JETS

**SPLAYED END 1:2
ELEVATION**

20mm RADIUS BULLNOSE TO SOLID SURFACE MATERIAL

3MM MOULDED SURFACE SIDE PANEL

SECTION E E

3mm MOULDED SURFACE SIDE PANEL

SPLAYED END 1:4

REV	DATE	DESCRIPTION	RISK	REV	DATE	DESCRIPTION	RISK	REV	DATE	DESCRIPTION	RISK	REV	DATE	DESCRIPTION	RISK	REV	DATE	DESCRIPTION	RISK	REV	DATE	DESCRIPTION	RISK
	14.04.97	ISSUED FOR PH2 CONTRACT		C	13.08.97	REVISED DESK JET & SUPPORT LEG																	
A	22.05.97	MINOR REVISIONS PRIOR TO CONTRACT		D	17.10.97	REVISED AND ISSUED FOR CONSTRUCTION																	
B	27.02.97	METAL TRAY, DESK JETS AND DESK LEVEL CABLE ACCESS ADDED																					

PROJECT 221 | NATWEST MEDIA CENTRE | CRICKET WRITERS DESK DETAILS (PH2/M/01) | 1:2 | 11.04.97 | F U T U R E   S Y S T E M S | 221/C/D/008D

57

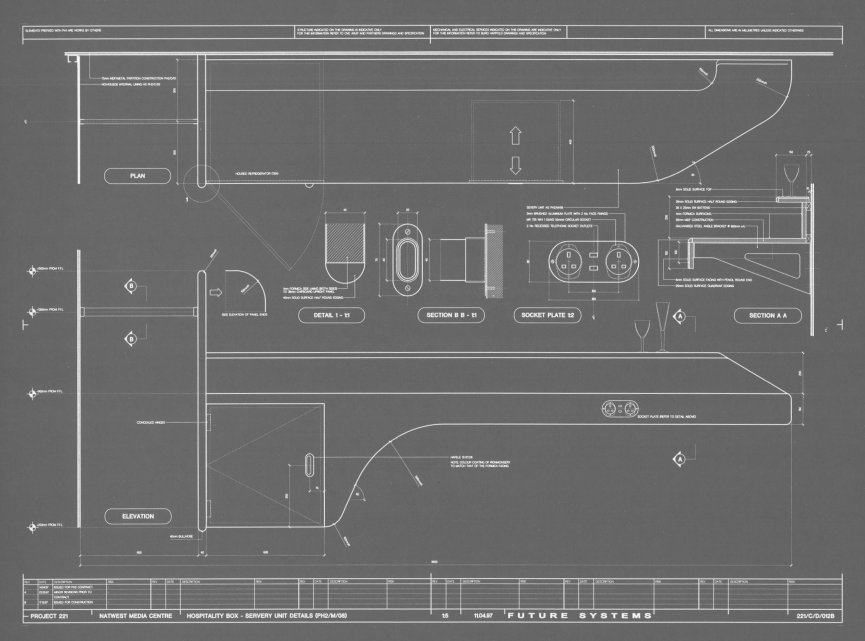

ELEMENTS PREFIXED WITH PH1 ARE WORKS BY OTHERS

STRUCTURE INDICATED ON THIS DRAWING IS INDICATIVE ONLY
FOR THIS INFORMATION REFER TO OVE ARUP AND PARTNERS DRAWINGS AND SPECIFICATION

MECHANICAL AND ELECTRICAL SERVICES INDICATED ON THIS DRAWING ARE INDICATIVE ONLY
FOR THIS INFORMATION REFER TO BURO HAPPOLD DRAWINGS AND SPECIFICATION

ALL DIMENSIONS ARE IN MILLIMETRES UNLESS INDICATED OTHERWISE

PLAN

HOUSED REFRIGERATOR (TBA)

75mm MDF/METAL PARTITION CONSTRUCTION PH2/D/01
NOVASUEDE INTERNAL LINING AS PH2/C/02

DETAIL 1 - 1:1

SECTION B B - 1:1

SOCKET PLATE 1:2

SECTION A A

SEVERY UNIT AS PH2/M/08
3mm BRUSHED ALUMINUM PLATE WITH 2 No. FACE FIXINGS
MK 735 WH 1 GANG 50mm CIRCULAR SOCKET
2 No. RECESSED TELEPHONE SOCKET OUTLETS

6mm SOLID SURFACE TOP
25mm SOLID SURFACE HALF ROUND EDGING
38 X 25mm SW BATTENS
1mm FORMICA SURFACING
25mm MDF CONSTRUCTION
GALVANISED STEEL ANGLE BRACKET @ 600mm c/c

6mm SOLID SURFACE FACING WITH PENCIL ROUND END
25mm SOLID SURFACE QUADRANT EDGING

1mm FORMICA SIDE LINING BOTH SIDES
TO 38mm CHIPBOARD UPRIGHT PANEL
40mm SOLID SURFACE HALF ROUND EDGING

SIDE ELEVATION OF PANEL ENDS

+1500mm FROM F.F.L.

+1000mm FROM F.F.L.

+500mm FROM F.F.L.

CONCEALED HINGES

SOCKET PLATE (REFER TO DETAIL ABOVE)

HAFELE 151.F2.18
NOTE COLOUR COATING OF IRONMONGERY
TO MATCH THAT OF THE FORMICA FACING

+250mm FROM F.F.L.

ELEVATION

40mm BULLNOSE

REV	DATE	DESCRIPTION	RISK	REV	DATE	DESCRIPTION	RISK	REV	DATE	DESCRIPTION	RISK	REV	DATE	DESCRIPTION	RISK	REV	DATE	DESCRIPTION	RISK
	14.04.97	ISSUED FOR PH2 CONTRACT																	
A	22.05.97	MINOR REVISIONS PRIOR TO CONTRACT																	
B	17.10.97	ISSUED FOR CONSTRUCTION																	

PROJECT 221   NATWEST MEDIA CENTRE   HOSPITALITY BOX - SERVERY UNIT DETAILS (PH2/M/08)   1:5   11.04.97   F U T U R E   S Y S T E M S   221/C/D/012B

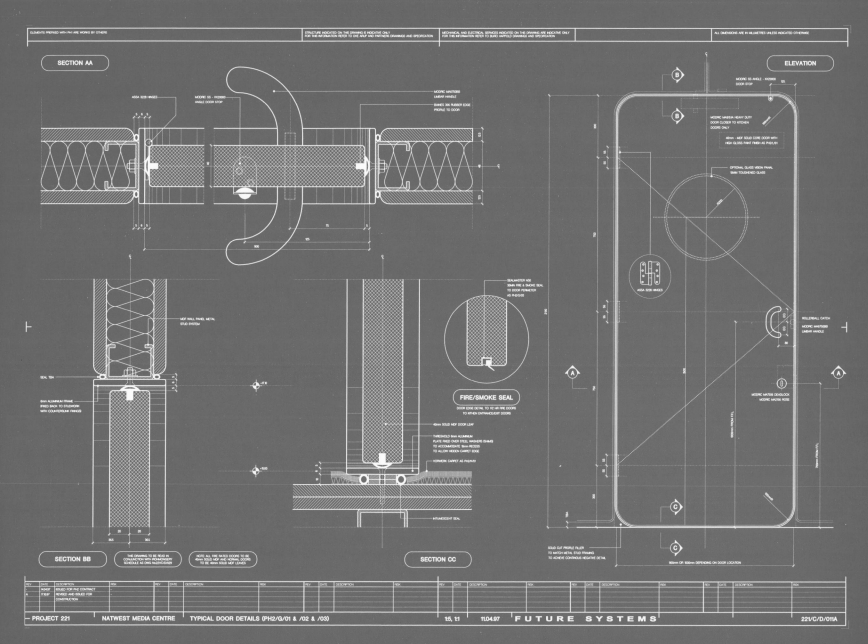

FIRE/SMOKE SEAL

SECTION BB

SECTION CC

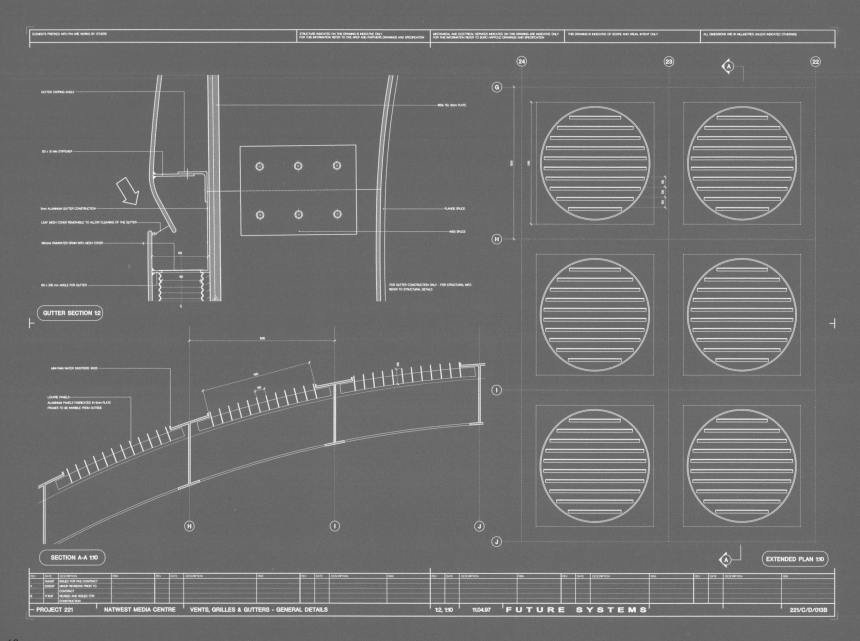

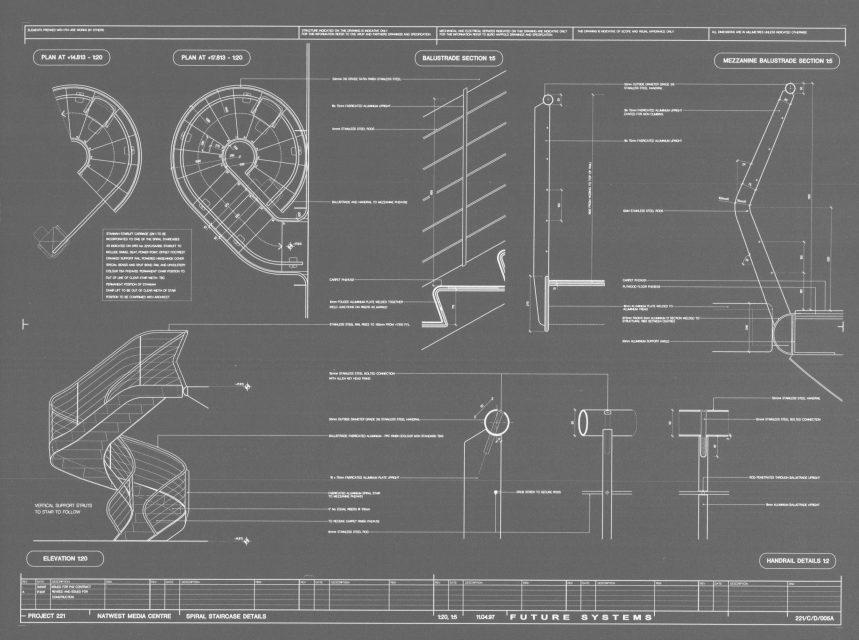

PLAN AT +14.813 - 1:20

PLAN AT +17.813 - 1:20

BALUSTRADE SECTION 1:5

MEZZANINE BALUSTRADE SECTION 1:5

ELEVATION 1:20

HANDRAIL DETAILS 1:2

VERTICAL SUPPORT STRUTS
TO STAIR TO FOLLOW

PROJECT 221   NATWEST MEDIA CENTRE   SPIRAL STAIRCASE DETAILS   1:20, 1:5   11.04.97   F U T U R E   S Y S T E M S   221/C/D/005A

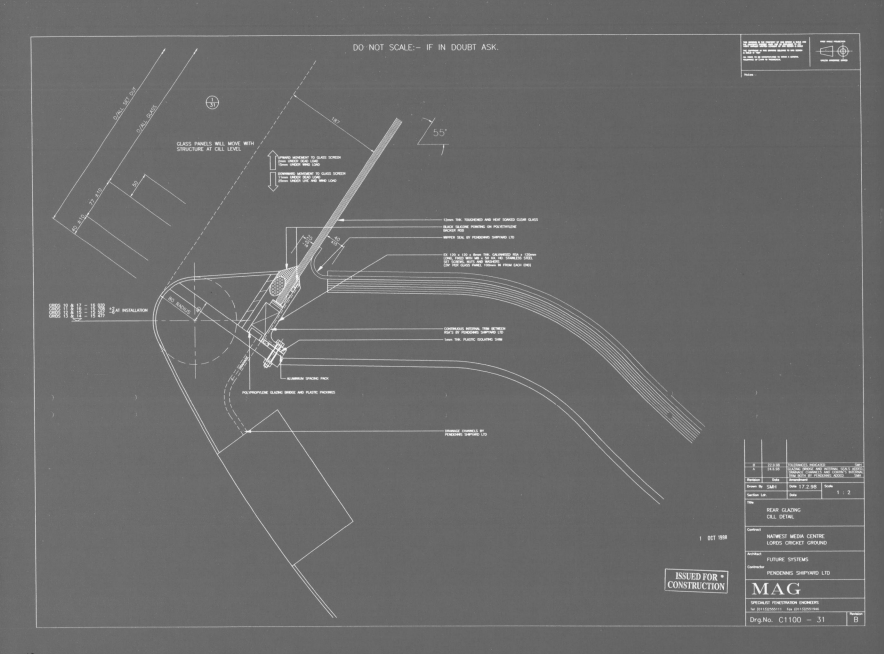

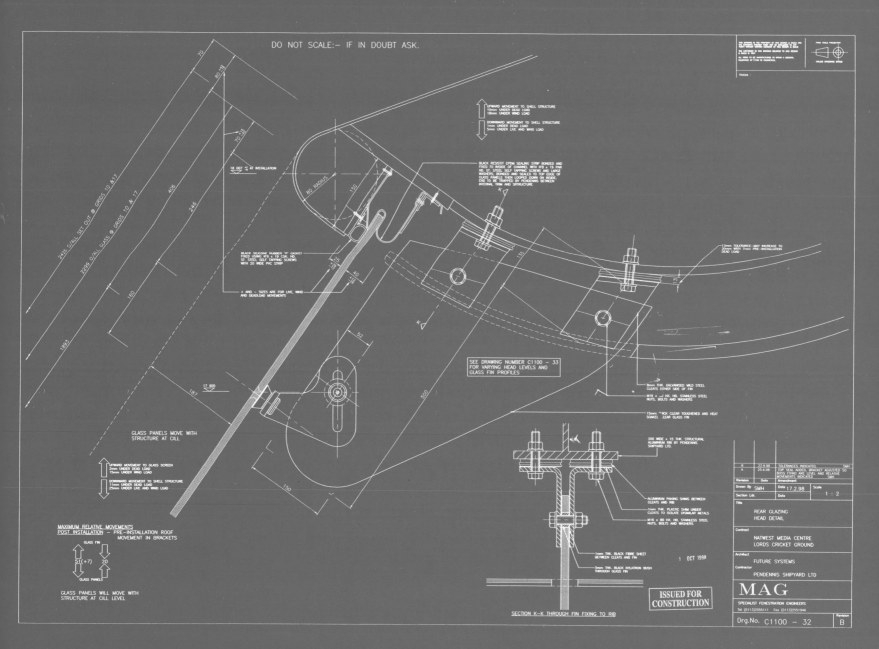

INTERVIEWS

Creating a building of any kind presents an incredible range of challenges to all those involved. To construct a dramatically different building in a prominent area of London, generally known for its conservative nature, gave all those concerned a taxing opportunity. The fact that the building stands majestically, at home yet individual and exceptional in its prime spot is a testament to all the players in the construction game. The Marylebone Cricket Club as the patron to such an architecture, the architect designers, the engineers all came together – albeit with a few sparks on occasions – to achieve this fascinating and inspiring building. Much has been written on the wonder of the building itself which is clear and evident to any observer, but the process of making it happen is an interesting tale of courage and innovation and adds to the intrigue of the building itself. The construction techniques, although commonly used in boat building, were new to the building construction industry. This meant that all those involved in the project had much to offer as well as learn from their colleagues on the scheme. We decided that the best way to communicate this story was in the words of those who were involved in the procedures and so we present here edited interviews about the story of the Media Centre. Clearly these are only a handful of the large number of people involved in the building of the Media Centre, but the cross section of interviews begins to build up the complete picture in a variety of dimensions.

MAGGIE TOY

1. Henk Wiekens, Partner, Pendennis Shipyard

MT: So what brought you to Cornwall after your stint of building boats in New Zealand?

HW: When we were in New Zealand, I was asked by an English designer if I would be interested in setting up Pendennis Shipyard for Peter de Savery, because he had this old docklands here, and *Blue Arrow* was about finished. He wanted an aluminium boat very similar to the one we built in New Zealand, but because he had all these people working here, he wanted it built in England. I came here in 1988 as to set up a group of people and build the boat. It was only going to be for 18 months – then I was going to go back to New Zealand. The 18 months grew to 24 months. By 1992 the property boom was over, and Peter de Savery couldn't really make the business grow any more. Then I got together with Mike Carr, who is my partner here now and who had come here from Vosper Thorneycroft in 1989. He and I put a plan together and bought the business out.

MT: How many projects do you have on the go at one time?

HW: About five. We try to keep three on the go, but it always ends up being five – so we keep needing more and more people.

MT: Are the boat projects bigger than the Lord's Media Centre?

HW: Not all of them, but they tend to have a bigger contract value on average. You have to remember that the Media Centre didn't need to float; it didn't need a mast, an engine room or a crew.

MT: How and when did you get involved?

HW: We had had an enquiry from Jan and Amanda, around the time we set up the company, when they needed some aluminium construction. The whole Media Centre was inspired by boat building and construction. When they were given the OK by the MCC – the building had been chosen as the number one option – we were asked if it was feasible and affordable and if we were interested in

making it. Mike and I went up for one meeting to their old office. I had heard about it a little bit through different contacts, and then I looked at the first drawings and the concept of what they wanted to do. You had to sort of fall in love with it, and if you didn't, you would have said, 'Very nice, good luck.' We said, 'Very nice, and we can do it.'

MT: So did you think it was feasible from that early stage?

HW: I never had a doubt. It wasn't that difficult. The difficult bit was convincing everybody else of that. We had a very early meeting here – the entire MCC committee came to see what we were doing. We had to convince them it was possible, and we only had three months to do it before they were going to have to make a decision, but these three months turned into 23 months.

MT: Were you particularly interested in architecture generally?

HW: Well, the thing about the Lord's Media Centre was a) it was a weird thing to look at, and b) it was Lord's cricket ground, the MCC. When we saw the whole concept of it and the involvement with such a one-off thing, that was the attraction for us. What came with it was that it was very high profile – it was in the centre of London, it had to be ready before the World Cup cricket, and it was quite futuristic.

MT: What was your contribution to the interior?

HW: We did everything – we were project-managing, and we sub-contracted everything out. There were no other contractors involved. We put up all the partitions, we sub-contracted the glass, and then we organised the steel for the glass to be fitted. We laminated it, we insulated it, we put in the mezzanine floor – that's aluminium as well – and the ceiling panels. We did all the electrical and mechanical systems – the air conditioning, everything.

MT: Was the cost ever an issue – did you have to cut back at any stage?

HW: Oh, yes. Cost was a major issue all the time. The original budget set out by the MCC for the engineering, electrical, construction and interior – everything except the concrete pillars – was something like £2.7 to £3 million. When we came to the process of tendering for the whole building we ended up doing a first estimate for certain elements of it – especially the aluminium, because the rest could be quantified by the quantity surveyors on behalf of the MCC. The only item they had a problem with was basically the aluminium construction. When we quoted that, the first round was based on 60 tonnes of aluminium – that was the original specification, and it was a lot more than was necessary. Then they finalised the design options – what the interior should look like – and what the mechanical systems should be. After that, we went through a phase of alterations. Originally the building was going to be naturally ventilated with a lot of open windows, and with a round window on the back that followed the curve of the building. In the end that window had to be flat, because the curved glass was too costly.

MT: You must have worked very closely with Future Systems on the design and costing challenges.

HW: In the beginning we did. They modified the design at certain stages, but the other people, like Arups, who were dictating other elements of the concept, always kept quite high and conservative on the specification. When we did the total pricing in the first tender round at Christmas 1997 or the beginning of 1998, we came up with a total figure of about £4.1 million for the whole package as specified. That was way out of their budget, so they said they had to revamp the whole thing. They were actually supposed to go to tender to several places with it. By that time we had already spent a whole year on it.

MT: It seems that you were almost sucked into it – first you were consulting and were asked to advise, and somehow you ended up doing the whole thing. Is this how you see it?

HW: Yes, it was a bit like that. But it's the same with the boats – we invest a lot of time making things viable and finding solutions for problems. We have quite a flat structure, and the people who own the company are also the people who make things happen, so we can quite quickly look at a problem from a technical point of view but also from a commercial point of view, and quite often we get involved more.

MT: It's obviously precisely because you work out how to answer apparently impossible challenges that you ended up building the Media Centre – you worked out the solutions.

HW: Absolutely. All the other people – except the architect – had major reservations about it. I had the impression that they all said 'yes' but all thought in their hearts that this was never going to happen anyway, so they were reluctant to commit themselves to putting in the effort.

MT: So how did the MCC finally agree?

HW: In the end, it got to the stage where we had to say, 'Forget it, we're not going to build it any more.' That's how we got the contract. We'd had the build-up through the whole of 1997, and they finally had the specification ready with a tender document so that we could give them a quote. That had to be done in December so that they could hand out the job in January. Then because the costing was way too high, they started slicing the budget. In January we had a meeting here in Falmouth with the MCC people, and were told that if we achieved a budget of £2.8 million we would have the job. The only way we could do this was to remove elements. We worked with the architect, and managed to get it down, but there was still no decision from the MCC. We wanted a clean two years with six months spare to have the job finished, and they needed it to be done by April 1999. We finally told them that if they didn't make a decision by 1 April 1997, it would be too late – we just couldn't fit it in professionally. The decision still didn't come. I was in Antigua when they started phoning up. I said, 'It's too late.' We felt really sorry for Jan and Amanda, but also for our own investment. Then the MCC really started getting worried. Maurice de Rohan, who was on the MCC, was the one who eventually got it back on track. He phoned me every morning while I was away, saying, 'We have to find a solution,' and I would say, 'Well, there isn't one – if I said we can do it I would be lying.' He phoned me one afternoon when I had just woken up, and I finally agreed to one more meeting. There was one big meeting at Lord's on 1 May 1998, with the chairman of the MCC and representatives of NatWest. Mike Carr and I went up to London. There were two scenarios that we could see to make it still happen: they had to get their skates on, and we needed more money. Then they decided 'yes'.

MT: How did you manage to get the costs down as far as you did?

HW: We did that basically by taking a lot of conservatism out of it. That building is incredibly conservative; it's never going to fall apart. But it's not necessarily a good thing for the concept – it's like making an ice-breaker to operate in the Caribbean. Over-specing wastes time and money. If we make a sailing boat to do 150 knots, we don't make it so strong and stiff and heavy that it doesn't do 150 knots.

MT: That's what struck me in seeing the interior of the aluminium boat that you're building at the moment – it's incredibly fine; the ribs are incredibly small. I assume the structure is as refined as it can possibly be, because obviously you want it to be light. But obviously, in the case of the Media Centre, Ove Arup are the engineers, so at the end of the day they have to take the responsibility if it falls apart – and of course there are no rules for doing a building in that way because it hasn't been done before. Maybe there needed to be a bit more collaboration between yourself and the engineer.

HW: I think that's true. One of the most difficult things was that there were so many add-ons in Arup's final design. The problem is that we do the whole thing like a lego ship – we can do a flat-pack of a whole boat. We cut under-water plasma. The more you can cut in one head, the more economical it is. If you have to do this process over and over again to add on bits and pieces, if you don't sort this whole tonnage of aluminium out in one hit, then the costs start to escalate. Anyway, we spent the whole summer cutting.

MT: Did Jan and Amanda ever doubt that you would get it finished?

HW: Oh yes. Even I did probably, if I admit it. It went through phases of problems, and everyone was getting worried about the schedule. But in the end we all had a bit of faith that it was going to happen – otherwise we wouldn't have done it. The worst thing was that all of us knew it had to be finished for the World Cup. It would have been a disaster if it hadn't happened in time.

MT: So how did the Media Centre compare to your usual boat projects in terms of the time it took?

HW: It was a long job. Rebuilds for ships can take from 18 to 22 months. We actually started on the Media Centre in the summer of 1997, and we were working on it for two years.

MT: What's the expected life-span of the Media Centre as far as its structure is concerned? How long does a boat last if it's built like that?

HW: The aluminium boats have one big disadvantage because if you have salt water and dissimilar metals with aluminium you get electrolysis, so it corrodes. Lord's Media Centre is not going to see salt water. The dirty air in London can affect the paintwork, but I think the aluminium structure of the building is there for life – until people basically get bored with it. Then you just cut it up, melt it, and make something else with it. You can recycle that whole building, right down to the last bolt we put in there, or the last piece of welding wire. You can't re-use the steel or the concrete, of course, but everything that is part of the aluminium structure you can recycle.

MT: I assume it took a lot of energy to build – more than most buildings, would you say, because of all the welding?

HW: No, it's quick. But it's only worth using that material if there are specific reasons for it – you don't want to make a square box. It could be for the sake of lightness – it could just sit up in the air, because the beauty is the skin. The skin is part of the structure. I think it could have been a lot better if there had been more time to optimise the design, as was originally planned, and go for a second opinion. But it's always like that – when I build a boat, when the thing goes in the water, I say, 'OK, if we had done this, and this, and this, it would have been much better.' Part of the problem in the case of the Lord's Media Centre was that we all underestimated certain elements of it because of the logistics. We underestimated the whole scale of it. The influence of people working at Lord's was underestimated. The amount of work left to do at Lord's was underestimated as well. Originally the idea was to build the whole building inside our shed in Cornwall, because it fits in one of the bays. We were going to fit the entire thing together, finish it all off in these units, prefit the glass, do the interiors, take it apart, have it all painted and then just dissemble the whole thing and set it up at Lord's, because the only time we had at Lord's was in between seasons. In the end, because there were so many delays in decision-making, that wasn't possible – we had to contract some of the work out, and when the first units went to Lord's we were still building the last ones.

MT: When did boats start being built out of aluminium?

HW: In 1903 – one of the Americas Cup boats, *Reliance*, was built half out of aluminium and half out of bronze. It only lasted three months, though – it wasn't very good aluminium. It was during the Second World War that they started to develop the use of aluminium, because they wanted to find non-magnetic metals and light materials – for minesweepers and that sort of stuff. It was developed in the aircraft industry – that dictated the use of aluminium. Then it was used for small craft. It wasn't until the 1960s and '70s that it was being used more frequently.

MT: What I'm driving at is when it became possible to use it as a building material. I think we're now at a stage where the next phase of architecture is going to be aluminium building – complex curved structures – because we've used boats as guinea pigs, and they've proved to work incredibly well.

HW: Well, aluminium is used in the boat industry, and we are already using other materials as well – composite materials like carbon fibres. We build whole boats out of carbon fibre, and they are even lighter – like the Americas Cup boats you have now. It's important that sailing boats be as light as possible.

MT: Do you think that method could come after aluminium – composite materials could be used for architecture?

HW: They are already being used – not as a structural material, but they could be used that way. Bridges now have carbon-fibre beams, and they are far lighter and stronger for their weight. Aluminium is strong for its own weight, so you get a big structural advantage. And it isn't corrosive. Composite materials don't corrode either. They have an even longer life-span. The only difference is that with composites it is a mechanical property – a man-made property – because a composite only works if you laminate it and if you inject a resin or whatever. That's why it's still not used on fuselages of big aircraft: they

can't guarantee the uniform strength of the material. In a boat you can over-engineer, because the weight is not as critical as it is in an aircraft, and if it cracks it doesn't fall to bits. If it cracks you can fix it, but in an aircraft you'd be down on the ground.

MT: But where do we stand in transferring this technology to building on the ground?

HW: Look at all the buildings when you walk through airports – at the non-ferrous materials used. Stainless steel rots; it's inevitable. The standing rigging that we use on the boats, with toggles and tie rods, is all over the building industry. It all comes from stainless steel rigging for sailing boats. But the shape of boats has been partly dictated by the materials available. These days boats can be a lot sleeker than they could before, purely because of composite materials.

MT: There is a similarity in architecture, where people keep trying for the ultimate.

HW: Look at football stadiums. There is not one pillar obstructing your view in new stadia. Modern materials make that possible, because they make the roof so light that the span can be bigger and bigger. The things they use for cladding are so light, but they still keep the water out. In the old-fashioned structures they couldn't have a roof material light enough.

MT: Are you working with any other engineers or architects?

HW: We are dealing with a few other enquiries, including an element for Blackfriars Bridge with Anthony Hunt Associates. Quite often now engineering companies approach us as well, because we can be quite a help to them. We haven't built anything for other architects yet. We were asked to make the modules for the London Eye, but we simply couldn't because of the time. That commission eventually went overseas – to France. Immediately after the Media Centre we got a huge number of enquiries – as soon as it was built everybody thought, 'What's in the bottom of my drawer?' So they all took out these crazy projects to see if I could give them a price. The problem is, we've had so many enquiries that we've had to be quite careful about which ones we pursue. If someone calls me with an idea, I ask them to come to see the boatyard, because if they can justify to their company taking a day out and spending £120 on a train or plane, they are probably being serious. If they're not prepared to make that effort and see how we work, I'm not interested in the project. If I bring them here and they like the atmosphere, we can work together. When they taste what is going on here, they start to take us for real.

MT: So would you do this sort of project again?

HW: Yes. It's been quite a challenge, and it's been a fantastic achievement for everybody involved. There are so many little stories that made the whole thing fun, and there are quite a few stories that made it a pain in the neck as well. There's no point for us in getting into the building industry, because we wouldn't be any good at it and it would just be copying somebody else. As long as it's different and there's something where we can apply our skills, then it becomes interesting.

MT: You say that there are some very interesting stories about getting it finished. Tell me some more of those.

HW: One of the hiccups that happened was when it was near completion. It was a few days before the opening, and the corporate PR people from NatWest came into the building. They had the two VIP rooms on either side, and all the carpets were in – everything was there. They walked into these rooms, and they went absolutely ballistic, because everything was as Barclays blue as you could get. So the carpet had to come out and it had to be green. The funniest thing is that we ended up getting a prize, the Cornwall Export Award for Cornish companies – the award ceremony was sponsored by Barclays, and we got that prize because we were building a NatWest Media Centre. When I accepted I said, 'Don't worry, I know it's the NatWest Media Centre, but it's your evening and you're the sponsors …' and all that sort of stuff. Then I said, 'Listen to this one' and I told them that story. It was fantastic.

2.   Brian Thornton, MCC Committee member

MT: How did you come to be involved with the MCC?

BT: I'd been a member since about 1960. I'm a great cricket fan, but not a player. My father had been a very good real tennis player – the old game of tennis. There is a court at Lord's and he thought that my brother and I ought to play as well and made us members. That was how I became a member of the club. I wasn't a cricketer, but I always loved the game. In 1985 the MCC decided that they needed to rejig their management structure. They split the responsibilities for estates from the running of cricket, by hiving off various areas to sub-committees, and each of these reported back to the main committee. The Arts and Libraries, as it is called – there is a marvellous collection of books and pictures at Lord's – was one of the areas that was hived off. There was a chap called David Mayle, who was one of the senior partners of Gardiner & Theobald. He was asked to be chairman of the Estates Committee, and he went through the membership list and selected people whom he knew who were surveyors, property developers, architects, engineers and so on to join him on that sub-committee, and I was one of those. It was then that the main committee said, 'It's the bicentenary of the MCC; we must do something here to commemorate this.' It was decided that the old Mound Stand at Lord's should be rebuilt. It was very dilapidated. The fact of the matter was that Lord's was in a pretty ropey old state. No money had been spent on it for years.

MT: Was that through lack of money, or lack of forethought by the people running it?

BT: I think it was a bit of both. It was partly the lack of knowledge by the people who were running it about how to maintain it. They were all cricketers, and the only thing that mattered was that bit of grass out there. Besides that, up to 1985 there is no doubt that one of the reasons that there had been a lack of maintenance was shortage of cash, but the membership had increased by that time, and there was a much more commercial approach coming in. We felt that the Mound Stand was probably in the worst condition and represented the best opportunity for increasing the capacity of the ground, so it was agreed that that should be the first thing we tackled. We had an architectural competition. There was one member of that sub-committee who was an architect, called Peter Bell. I have to say I think the responsibility for the way things have developed at Lord's in terms of the quality of the architecture is very much down to Peter. He introduced the Estates Committee to Michael Hopkins' as a sort of wild card in the competition. It was a very interesting experience when all the competitors put forward their proposals. There was very quickly a consensus that one of the commercial firms should be chosen, but then up comes Peter and says, 'I'm terribly sorry, but you've got it all wrong.' He was very good, because he told us why we'd got it all wrong, and he showed us why Hopkins' scheme was streets ahead of all the others. His was the only one that kept the original terrace that was there, which a) saved cost and b) made the job easier, because any work that's done at Lord's has to be done in the close season. This is one of the big problems of building at Lord's – it drives the structural solutions to whatever we do there. It has to be done in some sort of prefabricated form usually. The building was finished in 1987, just in time for the bicentenary celebration. To begin with, it was quite interesting: there were very mixed criticisms and views expressed, but as soon as that building started to be used and people realised how superb it was, everyone thought it was just magic. I think it was realised that high-quality architecture pays – not only do we help the image of the club by having superb buildings at Lord's, it also pays off. After the Mound Stand we had a pause, and then we did the Compton and Edridge Stands, which are the two little stands at the far end, underneath where the Media Centre is now. I think one must say that none of those jobs would have been done without the financial help of Paul Getty. Paul was a member, and he contributed a significant amount of the cost.

MT: Were the Compton and Edridge Stands the result of a competition?

BT: No, Hopkins was given those on the back of his performance on the Mound Stand. But an opportunity was missed in my opinion, because the height of the stands was restricted so that the view from the pavilion of the trees beyond them was maintained for the members. It meant that they were low and therefore the potential capacity was not realised.

MT: What is the total capacity?

BT: Now the capacity is 38,000. It used to be higher, because people were allowed to stand everywhere and sit on the grass, but then the Safety at Sportsgrounds Act came in because of all the horrors we had at one of the football gounds, so now it's an all-seater. Then the next project that came along was the cricket school. There had been one at Lord's for some time – I think it was the first one that was ever built. The MCC has always been a great supporter of youth cricket – boys from schools in London could come and train there. But it was an asbestos-roofed, porta-shed thing, and it was leaking, so we needed to do something to it. We had another architectural competition for that. It was Hopkins, David Morley and one or two others. David Morley's solution was brilliant. Again, Peter Bell had suggested that David's practice should be included. So we built the cricket school. Then David was given the ECB offices next door to do, and the little shop.

At that stage – in October 1994, I think – David Mayle stepped down as chairman and asked me to take his place. As chairman of the sub-committee, I was automatically on the main committee, as I had to report to them. The first thing the committee said to me was, 'We've got this World Cup coming up in 1999; we must have a new grandstand.' It was an enormously fun thing to do. We had a study done of the remaining stands at Lord's. One half of the ground was done by Nick Grimshaw and the other by Hopkins to find out how we could develop the rest of the stands around the ground. We picked on the grandstand to be done next because we could get more seats in. The potential was by far the greatest. And the old grandstand, which was a Herbert Baker building, finished in 1926, was dreadful. Over 40 per cent of the seats had obstructed views of the playing area. There was then a hullaballoo because people were saying that the building shouldn't be pulled down – that it was in a conservation area, and should be listed. To cut a long story short, English Heritage, to their credit, said: unlistable – because it didn't fulfil its function. And in fact the story is that Herbert Baker was going to be sued by the MCC when it was finished, and when he heard this, he came up with this weathervane called Old Father Time, and said, 'There you are; put that on top of the new grandstand, it will make it look lovely.' And they said, 'Oh, fantastic,' and

gave up. That's the way business was done in 1926!

Anyway, we had a pressing deadline, and I knew we couldn't spare the time for a competition. So I went to see Nick Grimshaw, and we agreed he was the right guy, and away we went. I said that it had to be built in two close seasons and he needed to do his design on the basis of getting it done by then. As you may know, it's steel and pre-cast concrete. It's lovely – I think everyone likes it. It doesn't sit quite as comfortably as the Mound Stand, because its footprint is very narrow and so it's rather stacked up. We increased the capacity by 50 per cent, and every seat has an unobstructed view. So that was that. But not long after I'd got going on the grandstand the next penny that dropped for the World Cup was the question of the media. The previous facilities for the media were pretty rudimentary. There was room for about 90 journalists, and the commentators were in little wooden shacks dotted around the ground. Tony Lewis was a member of the committee. He writes for *The Telegraph* and was the anchorman for BBC television commentaries. He's been captain of England. He had said in the committee, 'If we're going to have the World Cup here at Lord's we've got to do better than this.' So that landed on my plate in April 1995.

MT: That was four years before it had to be finished, then?

BT: Yes. It was agreed that we needed to put journalists and commentators together in one place and keep them under control! We needed to give them the most up-to-date facilities that we could afford. I was told that it had to be behind the bowler's arm, as that's the best place from which to view the game from. So it either had to go at the nursery end, where it is, or above the pavilion. We had a look above the pavilion, but it wasn't suitable because you can't get the sight-lines there; the pavilion itself gets in the way. We decided to have an architectural competition, because we had the time – it wasn't nearly as big a project as the grandstand. We selected David Morley, Lifschutz-Davidson, GMW and Future Systems. It was Peter Bell who said Future Systems were flavour of the month – they'd be our wild card for this time round. David Morley's scheme and Future Systems' scheme stood out from the other two. We had quite a long period – at least six to eight weeks – where we were weighing up whether we should go for David Morley's scheme at a cost of just under a couple of million, or this very futuristic scheme by Jan and Amanda which was going to cost at least two and three-quarters. David's scheme was very low-key in comparison to Future Systems'. I think you could say it respected Michael's two stands much more. It was more traditional. It had quite a lot of exposed steelwork staircases, which worried me – how are we going to look at those in the next 50 years? But of course, because of the difference in cost, the Estates Committee split, although there was a majority, which I was part of, in favour of the Future Systems scheme. I had the impression that this really would be a tremendous statement for the MCC – *if* I could persuade my colleagues.

MT: If the money had been equal would they have gone for Future Systems? Was it purely financial?

BT: No, definitely not. I would have said there was a view that the Future Systems scheme was too risky. Risky in many ways, not only the aesthetic solution, but risky in getting it done. But once I'd seen it I thought we would be able to do it somehow or other.

MT: At what point did you go to the boatyard? Because Henk Wiekens of Pendennis Shipyard was saying that that seemed to be the clinching point. He was able to say, 'Look, it's not that new; we've been using this technology for years in boats.'

BT: I think that was very important, but at that time, when we were making the selection, we in the MCC didn't know that Amanda and Jan had been talking to a boatyard. They didn't tell us that. I think they were probably concerned that we would not want to feel trapped into going for just one contractor. Our quantity surveyor, DLE, Richard Baldwin – and the rules of the club – said we must go out to tender, to ensure that we got a commercial deal. I was saying, 'I'm sure we could find somebody to do this, don't worry' – which was very naughty really. I was then confronted with taking the two schemes to the main committee and telling them that the Estates Committee was split. The then president Oliver Popplewell, the secretary and the treasurer all told me, 'No way. We don't like it.' Aesthetically they didn't like it, and they thought it was too risky. So I asked the president if I could present the situation to the main committee. I told them that I very much favoured the Future Systems solution. At the end of it all the president asked for a vote. He asked them to vote on the basis of the aesthetic solution only and to put out of their minds the difference in cost. Every single member of the committee voted in favour of it except those three, which is quite remarkable. Mind you, I'd had great support from Tony Lewis and Tim Rice, and I think several of them listened to their views.

So that was it. We'd got the committee to approve it, and I was able to tell Jan and Amanda that the job was theirs. Of course, they were absolutely thrilled. They were appointed in October 1995, so it had taken from April to October. It was very quickly realised that we were going to need support from a sponsor. We approached the Millennium Commission and they said 'no'. I think the Media Centre knocks the Dome into a cocked hat, but then I'm a bit biased! A big attraction for a sponsor would be to have a couple of corporate hospitality boxes in the Centre, and to do that we had to make it bigger. The brief changed, in other words – I think slightly unfortunately in terms of the shape of the building. It was originally more elliptical; it now has quite a flat top and bottom with rounded ends. Up went the cost automatically, so we were actually now up to about £3.5 million, and I was really sweating, but we were able to persuade NatWest to put in £2.6 million over five years. Then I needed to get the approval of the members, so I held an SGM – a Special General Meeting. I'd already had one on the grandstand and told them to spend £13 million. I was put on the spot at the SGM by the members: they wanted absolute assurance that it was going to cost £3.5 million, and I said it would, because I'd gone into it as best I could with DLE, and they'd said that was a safe figure.

MT: So how did the project develop once it had been accepted by everyone?

BT: There was then a long period of design development with Amanda. I get the impression that she manages the practice as she's the tougher one, whereas Jan is on the face of it rather a soft character, and I believe a brilliant designer – so the two of them make a perfect partnership. We had a design team of high-powered brains on it, because we had David Glover of Ove Arup doing the structural engineering – a brilliant man. I think Future Systems were under enormous pressure. They were a very small practice, with very few people, having to produce information out of a hat as it were, and I think they were also on very tight fees, as were all of the design team.

We had several crises. I stepped back from being chairman of the working party because I was so busy making sure the grandstand came out on time. One of my colleagues, Maurice de Rohan, who is a structural engineer, took over as chairman. The first thing he did, which was very sensible, was to say, 'This is a one-off building. Are we sure it's going to stand up?' He asked Ove Arup to have a separate team of their engineers check everything, at the end of which they said, 'It's fine.' But later down the road we found that we needed another 60 tonnes of aluminium to make it, because someone wanted belts and braces. Those were the sorts of crises that happened. It was during that time that, obviously, we began to talk about how we were going to get it built. The quantity surveyor, Richard Baldwin of DLE, suggested that we split the building so that the two pylons with the lifts and staircases and the foundations of them – they were just concrete – were one contract, and the pod was a separate one. Then we would build the two pylons in one close season – 1997 – and in 1998 we would do the pod. Because if it was all going to be prefabricated it would be a doddle.

It was at that time that Amanda started talking about how the right way to do this was to go to a boatbuilder. We all went down and saw Henk. We were very impressed with these marvellous boats he was building there and how he could bend aluminium, and weld aluminium, and do anything you like with aluminium. DLE was now telling us that really the construction industry was not interested. The decision was made to split it – Heery was going to manage Osborne's construction of the two pylons. Heery was also the management contractor on the grandstand, so that was quite straightforward. But the legs were another financial shock, because in fact the actual cost in the end was about £200,000 more than had been allowed for. How it came about I'm not sure, but I had to report this to my colleagues and I was getting more and more concerned.

MT: You must have had to get planning permission at some point?

BT: Yes – I'd always felt it would be a problem, but we used Hugh Bullock from Gerald Eve as our consultant to help us through the maze. On his advice, we had a press conference, and we ended up making the planning application in October 1996. That was a year from when we appointed Future Systems, so it was getting late and we needed to have the legs built in that close season – 1996–97. What was great was that the Royal Fine Arts Commission and Westminster City Council both said, 'Fantastic, we love it.' Only English Heritage said, 'We don't like the view from Regents Park.' But it sailed through, which I found quite extraordinary. So we dropped the flag with Heery, and off we went.

Then we had to go to tender for the pod. We insisted that we had at least three boatbuilders, and three contractors looking at it from a management point of view, so we got six bids in. The construction industry was hopeless, and of the boatbuilders we certainly got the impression that Pendennis was the only one who was going to be able to do it. There was tremendous nervousness in that situation, because we had the absolute deadline of the World Cup. Another problem that arose involved ordering the aluminium. Henk had reserved it for a good price up to a certain date, when he had to confirm the order, but at that time – early 1997 – Maurice de Rohan was taking over from me, and we managed to miss the deadline. That cost us an additional £150,000. I'm just trying to give you some of the reasons why this cost escalated. Now at that point I'd instituted with Amanda and the rest of the design team a complete run-through of how we could save money, because this was getting out of hand. We came up with several options: we wouldn't clad the legs, we took away the camera gantry underneath, we abandoned Future Systems' ideas of having glass doors for the commentary boxes, and replaced them with portholes. We also took lights out of the roof – we had been planning to have circular lights, which would have been lovely. Having done all that, we were late, and that cost money. It then transpired that Henk had already committed himself to build some more boats in the yard. It soon became clear that he hadn't got the capacity to assemble all the units in Penzance, so he had to have some of them done in Holland. I must say, all credit to him that he managed to organise the show and administrate it so that they fitted when they all came together. There was a huge extra cost for him in doing it like this.

MT: It is usually accepted that projects of this sort generally cost more than predicted. The fact is, you can have a good design, but if there isn't a patron who will provide the money and support it's never going to happen. I think everybody does recognise how brave the MCC was on every level. All the niggling about how much it cost and how it didn't actually need all that aluminium was in a way irrelevant.

BT: That's true – in the fullness of time I don't think the cost will matter, because the payback will always come. Anyway, we struggled away, and in fact I have to say I think Henk and his chaps did the most superb job. They finished in April 1999 in time for the World Cup, and it was beautifully done in terms of the quality of finish. The craftsmanship employed by boatbuilders is streets ahead of anything you see in the construction industry. I think the only problem we've got is the carpet. Generally speaking, the finishes in there are great, and we do our best to keep it looking pristine, but the carpet is hopeless – it's going to have to be changed. I think Jan said he'd got his inspiration for the colour scheme and the finishes inside from a 1962 Chevrolet or something. Suede coverings and pale blue. But the carpet is not something you see from the outside, and in every other way it's a triumph. None of the media have complained about anything, and the members' reactions have been very positive on the whole. It fits so beautifully with everything that's there already. But I was confronted at the Annual General Meeting about the cost, and I said, 'I'm very sorry, and I resign.' Everyone was horrified.

MT: But you won the vote to have the thing built in the first place with the chairman saying, 'Forget about the cost.'

BT: That was in a meeting of the committee only. I was put on the spot subsequently at the Special General Meeting by the members – and it's the members who own the place, it's not the committee – and I said, 'It will cost three and a half million.' Now, everyone says, 'You're mad; you shouldn't have done it,' but for me it's a matter of principle. If you say you're going to do something and then it doesn't happen, someone should take responsibility. I was the driving force behind this thing: I pushed it from day one, and I feel very responsible for what has happened financially. It's also fair to say that I'd done my stint, and it was time to hand over to somebody else. So it was really a gesture by me to say that it was my responsibility. I was absolutely comfortable doing that. I'm very proud of what's been achieved there, and it would be wrong of me to claim credit for all of it. There was huge support from people like Peter Bell and others.

3. David Glover, Engineer, Ove Arup Partners

DG: I've been a structural engineer for 22 years, and I've worked at Ove Arup and Partners for the last ten. I'm a director of the company, and I lead a multi-disciplinary group of about 80 people. We cover all the basic disciplines of building. We have structural engineers, mechanical engineers, electrical engineers and public health engineers in the one building. We fundamentally believe in total design in terms of how we approach our work. For the Media Centre, we were only commissioned to do the structural engineering, although the concept for the building was a multi-disciplinary approach. The concept was being dealt with by Andy Sedgwick, who's my fellow director for this group.

MT: What was your involvement in the competition for the Lord's Media Centre?

DG: I was not involved in the competition. I was in Germany, and I came back to work here just after it had been announced that Future Systems had won. We worked with Future Systems at that early stage, putting together concepts of designs for the Media Centre. The idea was always for a seamless form, but in every design process you always have to fight against something – cost, design suitability, buildability. Very early on, in the first six months, we had to put together the scenarios to show that building the Media Centre as a seamless form was the right approach. There were a number of issues that came to light. It was about proving the reliability of the aluminium solution. At that stage we involved Pendennis Shipyard: Henk Wiekens came down to the very first meeting. We had been working with several American Cup boats. There were a number of yachting engineers and naval engineers here who had been doing a lot of carbon-fibre work on boats, and we asked around to find who we should talk to about this project. Someone told us that Pendennis was a very good yard. All the boats are made of aluminium, and Pendennis are very focused and showed the enthusiasm that a project like this would need.

MT: Would you say that it was a passion for you as well, on the Ove Arup side?

DG: Yes, definitely. There's no way you could have delivered this project without total team commitment. Everybody had that same goal: to deliver this concept that we had found.

MT: Was the concept the same from the very beginning?

DG: No – in the early meetings we were doing detailed feasibility appraisals for two types of structure. We needed to ascertain what we thought it would cost to build the shell in aluminium, as a fully monocoque form, where the skin is used as a part of the supporting structure. But we'd also been asked to do some calculations on a steel skeletal frame – a much more traditional form of building – and we looked at how that would then be clad with a system. The problem with the latter is that the cladding is not seamless; it's jointed. It's called rain-screen cladding, and it's not waterproof, but it's put around – like tiles, if you want – and the waterproofing sits underneath the cladding. But to make these individual tiles and achieve a double curvature – the shell – particularly around the tight sides, you had to have quite thick aluminium to stop it looking wrinkly. Sheet aluminium is exactly the same as kitchen foil – if you wrap it, it wrinkles and creases. So we had to balance out whether it was worth using it structurally. As an engineer, you don't like to see good material wasted. We had that option costed by our quantity surveyors, DLE – but of course they didn't have a database for semi-monocoque structures, so we had to go to Pendennis for that. We went down to the boatyard and talked through a number of systems. It just so happened that there was a boat in the yard – a 35-metre-long motor launch – which was about the same size and volume as the Media Centre and had an aluminium hull. In a lot of ways there were similarities. They did some calculations that they don't normally do, to work out prices per tonne for manufacture in aluminium. We used these prices to work out the cost of the aluminium shell, and we compared that to the alternative.

There were also some key issues we had to resolve from the start. If you have an external skin, you have a thermal performance to get out of it as well; you have an acoustic performance, because it can't sound like a tin drum when it rains; and there is also a fire requirement – the average fire is 500–600°, and at 500° you'd have no aluminium structure left. What was interesting was that in trying to solve these problems we used a lot of our internal expertise – from our own fire department – and also from the beginning we had Henk Wiekens, who had obviously had to solve the same problem with boats. Bizarrely enough, we solved the fireproofing problem by finding a certificate that was 25 years old and had been used on oil rigs for years; it had been clad – fire-protected – successfully. It worked. Pendennis also fireproof all their engine department rooms. So really it was all a joint effort. In the end, there was only about a five per cent difference in cost between the two options.

MT: So how was the final decision made?

DG: Once we'd figured out the costings for both options, we presented them to the MCC working party. I always classify it as a milestone presentation in the project for me, because it was about taking the MCC with us on the boat-building route. We ran these parallel slide shows, to show the advantages and disadvantages of both options. We ended it by saying, 'We still think the aluminium shell is the right way. It offers an advantage because it can be prefabricated, so there will be less site work.' At that stage they wanted everything built out of season, so we had two six-month windows over the winter, which isn't the best time to be building. So there was a lot to be said for big prefabricated modules coming to site and being quickly erected, sealed and finished. We ended the presentation with them agreeing that that was the right way to succeed. We did have to take them to Pendennis Shipyard. We showed the MCC the technology that was there, and they looked at the big yacht which when we first saw it was raw aluminium and now had been finished and was floating in the dock. One of the big things about this project is that it is a one-off; it is unique, and the similarity with the boat-building industry is there – they always build one-offs. They also always use strange geometry, when you compare them to a builder. Consequently the building industry wasn't capable of taking on the Media Centre. It always rationalised it.

MT: I understand that you went out to obtain quotes from the building construction industry as well.

DG: Yes, we did. The MCC insisted on it. It's the client's prerogative – they have to be sure they're getting value for money. It was an informative exercise. There were some way-out suggestions such as alternative materials, but nothing that came in under budget. Substantially most of them reduced the risk of what we were attempting. Overall, when everything was taken into account, Pendennis was the best value. I wouldn't say cheap, because some others were cheaper, but they weren't the same quality. The value that was put on it was always circa £3.5 million. There's no doubt about that. The shell was about £1.4 million, so the structural core was that. At the end of the day that came in roughly on budget. I think what people forget about is that the final £5 million is a fully-fitted-out price – and, let's face it, the Media Centre is not a normal office fit-out. It's not just a box on stilts. It's beautiful – that's what you're paying for.

MT: Can you describe the basic structure of the building as it stands?

DG: It is made up of two main parts. The first thing is the legs that support the building, and then you've got the shell. They're integral, but they were actually built by different people. Pendennis only had responsibility for the shell; Osborne won the tender for the legs – they were already working on site on the grandstand. The legs, because of programming, had to be put in during the close season the year before, so you're talking about a very long programme if you think back to when we first started the design concept five years ago. The software we could have used to design the legs now just didn't exist then. For a structural engineer the building is strange because it's got an eccentric load – it's constantly wanting to tip over because of the way it hangs over the stands. The legs predominantly sit at the back. If you look at the section it doesn't look as though it's balanced, and it's not. The load sits right towards the front of the building. Consequently, the legs had to be pretty robust. They also had to act as a fire escape off the stands, power the lifts and act as the stair axis for the building, so they're quite fundamental. Again, they are not just two columns; they are a complicated set of individual components brought together. They are designed as tension piles, and they go down to about 26 metres below ground level. In other words, what stops the Media Centre falling forwards onto the pitch is the piles. They are actually very thin; thin walls with a steel staircase going through them, and the steel staircase helps stabilise the legs as well. At the level where the shell attaches to the concrete there are big, complicated steel plates cast into what we call the ring beam, which fundamentally holds the whole building up. A lot of design decisions had to be made even before we tendered Pendennis – we were committed at least seven to eight months before we tendered the shell. When we tendered and awarded the contract to Pendennis, we actually had a full design, but what was good was that I had agreed to pay Pendennis a lump of money early on as a technical adviser to help work up those designs and details. There were certain things about the spacing of ribs, the orientation, joining the shell, whether it should all be built as a big prototype in the shed – all of those issues we had to bounce off someone else. We had to balance our knowledge of building with their knowledge of ship building, and somehow bring out a tender that was workable. Now, as engineers we did the full design for the shell, so if a design element is wrong, we are responsible for that; Pendennis had a fabrication role in that particular aspect of the structure.

MT: I heard that there were some timing problems with Pendennis – that their appointment was delayed by the MCC.

DG: There is no doubt about that, and that is certainly what resulted in Pendennis being on site throughout the cricketing season. But it was a difficult situation because the cost for the building was more than was allocated in the MCC's budgets. That delayed the process, because people had to put in place those safeguards, and there is a constitution to follow. The MCC are unique, because they are adventurous; they have won all these awards for buildings. They are a very considered bunch of people – they can be frustrating, but at the end of the day they have still delivered an awful lot of buildings.

MT: Did you have to be a party to conversations with Jan and Amanda, and perhaps Pendennis as well, trying to convince them?

DG: No, it was a whole team. I think by that time it wasn't a question of convincing them that the solution was the right one. It was about trying to control budgets and over-runs. The MCC's buildings have a tradition of always going over budget, because there is a committee there, and someone says, 'It would be a nice idea to have that', and they're constantly upgrading. There's nothing unique about the Media Centre in that respect. People say that the original brief and the final brief are fundamentally the same, and they are, but the fact is that all the little bits make a big difference. When you make those decisions it has an impact on the cost. It's the same with any process we undertake as engineers. It's a difficult one.

MT: So you got to the point where the legs were up, and Pendennis was on board …

DG: Basically then we started what I call the beautiful process. People often say that the Media Centre is a totally wilful piece of architecture. I fundamentally disagree with that, because I think it's a rational response to the problems that were set out in the brief. The big idea for Jan was to have something that looks at the whole pitch and has a nice form. It does. You've walked around that site. From one side it is massive; from another side it looks minute. It changes all the time, and that's the beauty of a building like that. And it is a rational response, there's no doubt about that.

MT: But it was also, at least initially, using a construction system by which it didn't matter whether it was rectangular. That was the point. It wasn't trying to pervert something that is normally square and make it into a rounded form.

DG: Exactly. It was in the brief. The final shape, size and volume came from the brief – putting the brief down and arranging it in a very functional form, which is what Future Systems are absolutely fantastic at. They will take all these obscure requirements and arrange them really functionally. You go in there and it's clear where the writers go – you don't have to ask. If you want to eat, you can see which area to go to. Instantly you gravitate towards it. It's just right, and that's what's so rational about it. I'm not sure whether Jan likes to know it's a rational building. I think he associates that with too much rigour, but I think it's one of his great strengths. He can take typical problems and break them down and rebuild them up to a rationale that is still beautiful and works. The beautiful process was to do with understanding the concept, and the fact that the whole shape came from the brief. For me as an engineer, that's wonderful, because by that time we had already ourselves established for ourselves from the initial calculations, by computer and by hand, that this shell didn't actually work as what I would call a pure shell-type structure. This was because (a) it was supported at two points – you don't support shells at two points; you cut shells and support them on a multitude of areas, and (b) the form was very compact – it had been squeezed to give those 9 metres, and, if you look at it, it's got a very flat top and a very flat bottom with very highly curved edges. Now because it has a flat top and bottom that means it is acting very much like beams rather than an eggshell-type structure or a pre-cast concrete shell somewhere else. So we had to formulate and analyse the shell, which was seamless. That was very important, and we generated at that early stage, with the architects, a basic skeletal computer model. The beauty of it was that once we'd got the shape and the form right, that model went right the way through the project. It was the bit that everybody hung everything off. You had this one central core to the whole project that enabled this thing to work. It was about dealing with a complicated geometrical shape, realising we were into cornerless geometry. For a design process that was a fundamental key. We're actually doing that now on a number of other projects – we are using this same basic skeletal process to hang everything off. An early model showed that the aluminium plate contributed about 20 per cent towards the strength of the building: unlike a steel frame, where the beams just do everything, the plate was actually fundamental to the bracing; it formed the top flange of any one beam. So we also had to find out how to do that. People like Ian Feltham played a major role in that. He went back to basics. He analysed plate and buckling methods. We worked out how tight the curvature of the plate could be before a plate would buckle.

MT: When you say 'going back to basics', were you going back to basics because this hadn't been done before, or were you going back to basics in setting up new codes?

DG: Back to basics in the sense that we went back to the raw theory that they came from, because codes are an amalgamation; they're guides. Codes are practice; they are British Standards. There is a section that says, 'This is how you design aluminium curved plates', and there is one that says, 'This is how you design a plate that is flat', because everybody can understand that. But when you curve something it takes on totally different characteristics in terms of stiffness, what it will take as load and where it will be weak. We had to go back to all of those and basically draw up constraints on how we would analyse it. We actually wrote a post-processing routine that took all the raw data by computer, ran it and then re-spat it out in graphical form so that you could look at it. Instead of having to plough through all our data and find out where there were problems, that allowed us to start saying, 'There's a problem here, here, here and here.' Again, we had to write that from scratch. We ended up having to speak to the code-writing committee, because we didn't understand what they were trying to say. We thought it was not correct, and sure enough they had to agree themselves that, yes, we were right; it was wrong. That's because it's not infallible. It's not because they've made a mistake; it's because that's the process. Tools and analysis methods change. We've always required those processes to do that, but the only way we could do something like the Media Centre was to analyse. We had something like 42 load bases to consider, and the thermal expansion of the building, which in itself is an interesting concept. People say, 'It's white.' It actually had to be white because if something's white the maximum temperature it can get to is about 58°. If it's grey it can go to 90°. If it's black it can go to 120°. Normally if a piece of architecture is 38 metres long, someone will say, 'No, you've got to cut it in half and let it expand.' We've got 38 metres, by 12 metres, by nine, and there's not a join in it. When it heats up, this building actually swells – that's a feature of the shell. The heat doesn't get taken out in any one place; it just swells quite happily around a centre point.

MT: There is a big rain-slit all the way around – does that help the expansion?

DG: No, the rain-slit is there purely because of the rain. Again, that was positioned on the basis of studies that we had done, not exclusively for the Media Centre but on how long rain hangs onto something when it's at an angle. You usually find it will run down something at about 15° back on itself before it starts to drip off. As you will realise, the Media Centre is a big area and you can't have water dripping on people, so the gutter had to come in. It is a seamless gutter that is built in. The strength of the system is not broken at that point – the forces are all designed to go round the gutter, so that that gutter is actually a structural gutter. If you think about expansion, the building is shaded, so it's only the top of the roof that gets hot, so basically the thing will swell through only one side. In the model we analysed it, and you could see that the whole model literally swelled, and for a 2-millimetre movement at its roof and sides, you release all the forces that are locked into it. It was very important how we connected it to the legs. For example, the roof is actually sitting on top of the concrete legs, but they are on totally free-rolling bearings; in other words, it can move in any direction, so it's not constrained at all. As it cools and contracts, the roof moves in a number of directions. It tends to move diagonally because of the way the curvature around the back works. All of that had to be worked out so we were satisfied about where we wanted it to go.

MT: All these are points developed from your 'back to basics' philosophy. Doing this for each new project must be part of the enjoyment for you.

DG: It is, yes. It's an important aspect that people are frightened to do. I don't think you do it every time. There are lessons that we learned doing the Media Centre and subsequently applied on other jobs. So it's a continuous development process. Engineering's a bit of a strange thing. If you look at the history of engineering, there's not a lot that's new. What's new is the way we analyse and the way we use the material. That's what's making a difference.

MT: Would you say that's the same with the Media Centre then?

DG: Yes. I think the innovation is bringing together all of those bits of the jigsaw into one package. Actually, the building industry could not have built that building, whereas the boat industry could. But Pendennis couldn't understand the concept of building control, because they are controlled by Lloyds Register shipping. They get a representative to come down, and he says, 'Yes, that looks all right. Thanks.' And it's done.

This is clearly very different from the Building Control operation. There was a massive culture shock between the two. If anybody were actually to say – and be really honest about it – where all the angst came from, it was more because of that misunderstanding. It was our having to deal with nine million pages of Construction, Design and Management rules and issues – filling in risk registers and things like that. I'm not saying CDM is wrong; the rules are important, because they are there to save people's lives, but there is a balance. I think it was Henk who said, 'I don't think I've ever lost anybody in any of my jobs anyway, so I think I do it right.' We'd say, 'Yes, but you've got to sign a piece of paper to say you've done it right.' My perception of a boat, for instance, is that it creaks and is designed to certain limits. If it goes wrong, a plate pops off and it sinks, and people very rarely find out about it or they just mend it. In the building industry there is a totally different expectation. We, as engineers, very rarely design to strengthening criteria; we design to serviceability state. If the writers' area bounced up and down too much, that would be a major issue. They would complain about it. Henk would say, 'There's far too much aluminium in there,' but the aluminium was there to stop it bouncing up and down and not always to do with the strength. But then there were other areas of the building that were actually designed to their strength limits, and we felt comfortable about that.

MT: Is there anything you would do differently if you did this project now?

DG: We'd certainly analyse it differently, because we're now four years on and have different tools and a different approach. We've developed new computer programmes. There are parts of the job – parts of the fabrication – which, if you look at them now you can see are wrong. We knew they were wrong when all the bits arrived from the yard and they started to put them up. But to Henk's credit, he got on with it and did it. In the beautiful cold light of what the initial concept was, we never achieved that initial concept. There's no doubt about that. But there were lots of things that were unique in that building, and I think they were 70 per cent successful, and that's a fantastic success rate.

MT: Do you think the building industry – and perhaps your work particularly – can learn more from ship building?

DG: Oh, a tremendous amount. I think there are two things that are fundamental. Ship building is a high-craft, high-technology industry; building is far from it. Building is entrenched in lots of materials arriving on site in plastic bags and boxes. There is no apprenticeship, there are no skills, and there are no crafts. They are few and far between now. What's interesting about the boat-building industry is that you had a welder and a fitter right there – they were rectifying problems as they were doing it, and that high craft content is essential. The building industry has lost that over a number of years. It has become totally component orientated, and I think we need to learn from that that the future is not in component orientation. Components have their place, but not at the expense of everything else. There's also the matter of paperwork. Is it beneficial to the process or does it just add cost? There is a right balance, and we are always trying to achieve this. I think the innovation is bringing together all of those bits of the jigsaw into one package.

MT: When you first saw the Media Centre, did you think it would win the Stirling Prize?

DG: Yes, I did actually. I knew it would be unique. I knew it could be done, but I knew it couldn't be done as it was conceived on the original piece of paper. The thing is about how you go from the initial sketch to getting it solved. That is the process. I could see the solution; I could see ways of making it happen, but at that instant you don't know how. You don't know what the route is, but you just know there's a route there. And I think we had the controls in place to make it work – well, touch wood. We put those in place to make sure it worked.

4. Peter Bell,
Architect, Former MCC Committee member

PB: I'm an architect, and I've run a private practice here for years. I used to be in partnership with Richard MacCormac and Frank Duffy, both of whom became presidents of the RIBA. We separated because we had no work at one stage, and we were all bringing up children – that was at the end of the 1960s. I ran a practice from downstairs. Then a new assistant I had employed introduced me to tennis at Lord's. It's fantastic – these days I play two or three times a week to keep fit.

I was asked very early on to join some committee because I was an architect. We were building some new offices and squash courts on the premises at the time. They commissioned a scheme from some architects who are now called EPR (they were Elson Pack and Roberts in those days). I was pretty angry, because it didn't make use of all sorts of possibilities. The Tennis and Squash Sub-committee were anxious when I pointed this out, so I got seconded onto the Estates Committee, which was chaired by Colin Stansfield-Smith, who is a terrific architect. When he gave up he became a vice-president or vice-chairman of the RIBA, but he was already a Hampshire County Council architect, and he got far too busy, so he stood down. He was replaced by David Mayle, who later became president of the Royal Institute of Chartered Surveyors. They decided to amalgamate two committees and make David chairman of the new joint committee. Where most people given that job would think, well, I've got 15 people here and 15 people there, and I've got to weed some out and amalgamate them, he took not the faintest bit of notice. He went to the library, looked up the membership list and chose 15 new people. I was very lucky to survive – I was the only one from the original 30. He just chose people who could get things done, so we ended up with a fantastic committee (although we didn't know too much about cricket!). By that time, the place had been neglected for 20 years.

MT: There was a lack of understanding about maintaining it properly?

PB: Yes – it was hopeless. Actually, it looked like a very tired British public school. It was 20 acres of absolutely prime land but, as Neville Conrad pointed out, 20 acres is only worth what you can get from it. If, like in Hyde Park, you can only rent deckchairs, it isn't actually very valuable. Lord's was the same, but there was no reason for Lord's to be valueless. It was only used to its full extent on half a dozen days a year, but it was used on and off for all sorts of other things. As an Estates Committee, we had it in mind to improve the place, and some. The first thing we did was to decide to replace the Mound Stand. I persuaded the committee to have an architectural competition. I went on holiday and I came back to this list of six very commercial architects that the committee had chosen. I hadn't even heard of most of them, and I couldn't possibly approve of any of them. I decided to put up six myself. All 12 architects sent in their brochures. They were all laid out on one long table. We whittled it down very quickly by a process of elimination and asked three of them to come up with proposals. The point of the scheme was to knock the stand down and rebuild it at the end of the cricket season before the next season. In his presentation, Hopkins said, 'I've spoken to Doug Insell [a famous cricketer], and he says the best seating in the ground is this stand you're going to knock down! And actually it's a very nice stand, apart from all the modern stuff – the roof and the horrible way it stands on the wall at the back. If you look at the seating it's in a very good amphitheatre with perfect sightlines, occupying this third corner of the site. By extending the two brick arches that were there around and onto the back wall, and taking out the ghastly steel and replacing that with retaining walls you would have a really good stand. I'm going to propose to do that in the first year.' Eventually they accepted the idea – Hopkins won the competition, and we built the scheme. It cost just under five million – exactly twice the budget. I realised that every major project is done with all sorts of people knowing all sorts of things that you don't know, and that actually the budget wasn't terribly important. They knew all along that it would be successful financially in the long term.

When that was finished, the Estates Committee had gained a lot of credibility, and after that the main committee listened to what we said. David Mayle was also made president of the RICS, so they felt they were backing a winner. There were two other stands at the edge of the ground, Compton and Edridge, dreary old stands that were falling apart. We had no bother getting Hopkins in to redo them, and he did them beautifully. It wasn't a competition – no one questioned it.

The next project was to replace the cricket school – it was an appalling chocolate-brown-painted asbestos shed in the corner. Again, we were perfectly happy to get Hopkins to do it. He came back with a perfectly good design. It wasn't revolutionary, but it was a really good, competent building. But half-way through – we'd finished the design stage and were just about to submit it for planning permission – Ian McLauren, who was on the main committee as well as the Estates Committee, influenced the main committee into making us go to competition. We got five or six people. I had an assistant working for me who suggested including David Morley. He was the job architect for Foster's Renault building in Swindon. So they all produced schemes, and the three of us who were judging it – Brian Thornton, who's a builder and project manager; David Mayle and myself – were fortunately in total agreement that Morley's was much the best scheme. It was absolutely head and shoulders above the others, so that was a very easy decision. So that went ahead and was very successful. It came in on time and on budget. He's a very adept operator, and an extremely good designer. It was partially day-lit, and there were no shadows. It was a really competent piece of work. So that went smoothly, and we now had two buildings under our belt and even more credibility.

My intention was to keep the ball rolling and just replace the whole place. At that time it was on the cards that Lord's would get the Cup series, and we knew that we had hopeless media facilities, so this was an excuse to get the best media facilities possible. It would clinch the World Cup, so we were very keen on doing that. If the Oval, for instance, had stepped in and produced fantastic media facilities, someone could have made a move that it would be hosted there. So it was pretty easy to persuade everyone to do a wonderful media stand. It was obvious where the media stand should go. It wasn't to go above the pavilion, which is Grade I listed; we'd never have got the facilities properly there. Obviously it needed to be at the opposite end, because apparently behind the bowler's arm is the best place. We

set out on the North Stand and the Media Centre almost simultaneously, knowing that they were going to happen. Grimshaw was commissioned for the North Stand and, as he is a very skilled commercial operator, he very swiftly got the bulk of the money, leaving about two or one and a half million for the media stand, which was never going to be enough.

To find an architect for the Media Centre we held a competition. We were on a tight programme, so we didn't want a long lead-in process. Grimshaw had just done something, and there was also YRM – they always showed promise but they didn't deliver anything we could use. By this time we were very pleased with David Morley. He came back with a scheme that looked like the superstructure of a Second World War battleship. It was a very workable utilitarian answer, but I pointed out that it only worked for six days of the year. Future Systems came back with a scheme that worked just as well for all the facilities it had to provide for those six days, but that could be used all year round – it was basically a one-way-looking conference chamber with restaurant facilities on the same level. It was just a really useful adjunct to Lord's cricket ground. I had no doubt whatever that it would cost too much. Every building we do costs too much. As you go along you ask for extras, and the quantity surveyors all along the line know that if they admit to the real price it won't get built. But we took on Future Systems with great excitement. There were a number of us who were very confident about it and a number who were distinctly anxious. Future Systems had a very tight budget, they'd got an astounding scheme, and they'd got the same cost controllers that we'd had on all these schemes – D&L. The architects can't be blamed for the fact that it over-ran the budget – they design as best they can, it's costed, and it's accepted or not on the basis of the cost advice.

MT: The only people who knew how to do it were the ship builders, and they'd never built a building. It was all new to everybody. Was the aluminium the only area of extra cost?

PB: Oh no, there were loads of them. First it was the foundations, then it was the extra aluminium. Then we went out to competitive tender to boat-builders, not the construction industry. But the boat-building industry is much better organised and knows exactly who's in the running and who can do what. When everyone knew that Pendennis was in it they basically all backed off. The point is that the price we got wasn't competitive as such. But we were keen to build this building, and we were terribly keen to use Future Systems. We probably knew it was going to cost too much, but the money isn't important. We were doing something worthwhile, so I never lost my nerve on prices at all. We got the building up and we worried about the finances later. Lord's isn't going to go bust. Anyway, as I pointed out to the committee, St Paul's Cathedral was 35 years late and two times over budget, so who cares? I think Future Systems is showing us a way of building that's incomparably better than what we're used to. Their attention to detail was stunning. They're interior designers as well. They presented their building with all the interior fittings, down to the matching blue lavatory paper. It was smashing.

MT: Were you involved in all the logistics of getting it built on schedule?

PB: I was on the working party, but Brian Thornton was extremely good at that. He ran it very efficiently. We chose a fantastic team – we chose Future Systems, and they came with David Glover of Arups, who is a seriously good engineer. I'm off the Estates Committee at the moment. I'll try to get back on, because what I'd like to do is try and get somebody like Future Systems to make something that will quickly cover the place. If I had my way we'd be able to cover it in minutes – I don't give a hoot what it costs – so that we didn't have to stop playing. The Rolling Stones are coming to London – why not blow a cover over the whole thing and use it for a concert? Why go to Wembley? Wembley's out in the sticks. If the MCC's going to get commercial at any point, they should be thinking of covering the place to do a variety of things. It's 20 acres of central London! There's still a lot to change: there are six stands that we still haven't replaced, and a lot of forward vision is needed. In the end the MCC sense that the ground is pretty smashing and getting even better.

5. Jan Kaplicky, Partner, Future Systems

JK: When the MCC first approached us, it was not in a competition situation. We were already working on a screen for them, and they wanted us to design a secondary centre for the press, to supplement the area that the media were already using. It started off quite small, but it kept growing in size – throughout the competition and even more afterwards. So the first sketches are on one column only and very small.

MT: So, as the project developed, I assume the MCC decided to open it to competition.

JK: That's right. That, I think, is fair for something so important. They announced the shortlist of four people. Only Future Systems and David Morley got through to the second stage. That was quite a success and a great anxiety, of course, for us. We'd done two sets of drawings, but from day one the original idea was there, and it didn't change much. So we submitted again, and finally Brian Thornton phoned me and asked me to supply the data. The result of the conversation was that it had been accepted by the committee, and so we started.

MT: Did you know anything about cricket before you got to do the building?

JK: No, I knew absolutely nothing. I listened carefully to what Tony Lewis said in those first interviews with the television and the writers. I think that's a far better technique than pretending you know, or that you learn so fast, because you don't. You'll put the emphasis on the wrong things. They'll tell you immediately what is important. I'll always remember the importance of seeing both sides of the rope.

MT   How did the project develop once you'd won the competition?

JK: It was a very slow process – I never expected it to be such a complicated story. A lot of time was wasted in meetings where there wasn't even any discussion about the basic structure. I think it's partly because the press has created such mistrust of the professions of architecture and engineering that these days there's so much more bureaucracy. Instead of trusting the architects, engineers and quantity surveyors, you have to involve project managers as well. They kept delaying decisions and changing the parameters all the way through, and the fact is that every change involves immense penalties in terms of time and money. It was also very frustrating that we didn't get to talk to the press and television people. But luckily there were people like Tony Lewis, who has had a longstanding career reporting on cricket. In the end, he stopped all the criticism. He went around the building with some other person, and said, 'That's fine!' Then everybody stopped. I'm very grateful to him for that. There was peace and quiet, and it went through with flying colours at the World Cup. And I'm sure it will do so again this season and in many other seasons to follow. The important story is what was achieved by many hundreds of people. I will always remember the last welder who was sweating somewhere in Holland putting two sheets together. It was so impressive. I'll never remember some meeting, because it's too unimportant. The building works, and that's it. The media people love it – the comfort they have now as against the lack of comfort before … they couldn't even make themselves a coffee. They had mullions in front of them. One thing I promised them from the very beginning was a glass wall with no mullions at all. At that time I didn't even know it, but a new regulation came in, and we had to use not just toughened glass but laminated as well. But there are still no mullions. Nothing like that is used. They have 40 metres of glass. No other structure will have that.

MT: Did you have people other than Pendennis saying they could make the building?

JK: Yes, a German boatyard, but they lost interest very early on. It was difficult. For contractual reasons, along with pressure from the MCC and the project managers, who didn't have trust at all in the whole thing because it was so new to them – we were pressed to go to the building industry as well. There was talk about an internal skin – thank goodness we didn't have something like that, not just because it would be a different building, but because I would wake up every morning worrying about the membrane being penetrated and not possible to access, or leaking and this and that. Our basic concept was there from the very beginning. I think one has to praise Pendennis's understanding and wanting the challenge to do it; they were interested, Henk particularly. So the competition was over, and that was the beginning with the boatyard. That was the critical moment when we were pressed to use techniques that would be unsuitable for the type of architecture we wanted to achieve. The shape is not aerodynamic. The reason for the shaping of the building is very important: that it looks much, much smaller than it is.

MT:	Was that a planning requirement?

JK:	No, that came from Future Systems. I think very early on Amanda and I were clear that we didn't want to put another 'building' in that area. There were plenty of buildings around. We always thought about it as a 'camera' overlooking the site and having that as its object. We tried to make minimal impact. That proved right, because nobody ever complained about the size of the building, although it grew and grew all the time before our eyes as they added more and more people to use it inside. There was no problem with height. They said, 'It will be enormous, Jan,' and I said, 'No, don't worry.' And since then, nobody has ever complained about the size of the building. It actually looks tiny considering there are 300 plus people inside.

MT:	Yes, that was my first thought when I went there – it does look very small. It's like a Tardis effect.

JK:	Well, it's physical reality that a round object looks smaller than a box. If you had a box of the same capacity you'd be astonished. Aside from that, everything in cricket is round; nothing is straight: the helmet, the ball, the bat. The height was not dictated by us but by the view-lines of the rope from inside. Fifteen metres was dictated by circumstances, and quite rightly so. That's the whole purpose of the building. The glass wall in front had not to be straight for particular reasons – reflections, and so on. We had it tilted at 75° so that it wouldn't reflect on the players. One thing that was very important for me was to have no detailing at the top, so the only detail is the gutter. You have to legally satisfy the building controls and show that it will work. The gutter is a copy of that on the edge of the boot of a car. The only other penetrations on the roof are for the plant rooms. That was another breakthrough that was almost accidental. The plant rooms are open to the weather. They are like a huge bucket. You let the weather go in. Rain or snow go through, and then you drain the bucket. That is very important because you don't need the louvres, with which you worry about how much rain will penetrate the building. You don't worry about that. That's a very important detail as well. So there's virtually no obvious detailing. There are no masterpieces. The architectural magazines are very disappointed, because you can't supply a detailed penetration of the glass or anything like that. The major detail is so invisible, and that's the only detail I want to publish much because it's so simple that nobody believes it's there, because it's not painted over, and it will never show. That's very important. The smooth effect of the object in that rather busy environment was important from day one.

MT:	How did the design process between you and Amanda happen?

JK:	The main decisions are taken together. There are moments where effectively she is dealing with the client. I can't do that well at all. That's her speciality. Sometimes the designing is done in isolation – in the morning something comes. Sometimes some scribble is more important than real drawings. The process is very bizarre. Architects like to say that there's a sketch and it's somehow genius. It's not like that. It depends on another model, another plasticine, another polystyrene, another loaf of bread, as we used to call it. That all matters.

MT:	Is it designed very much from a plasticine model? Would you say it was more plasticine model than computer to arrive at that form?

JK:	Yes, there is no point in denying that. They do it in other professions as well. Every car is designed in plasticine, and there is a freehand drawing of the car. It's a fantasy that it somehow pops out on the computer screen. There were a variety of computer programmes involved – including ours, Arup's and Pendennis's, which goes automatically to the forming of the sheets of aluminium – and at one point even these were not enough. Average architecture and average engineering still don't have programmes that can map the whole structure of such a complicated object. That's relatively simple, but not in terms of manufacture. Identifying four corners of a sheet of aluminium is a hell of a process.

MT: So the form-finding was done between several professions, and you finally get to a stage where you've all agreed on what is the absolute optimum.

JK: Yes. And you can't draw it, because it's all a series of points in space. Yes, we can draw elevations, but in a certain way they are meaningless because you draw the register of the outline but not the space inside and outside the building.

MT: There must have come a point where you had to communicate to the MCC that this was the perfect shape. Did they accept that?

JK: Sure. We showed them the models, and that was enough for them to understand. I think one of the amazing successes of the building is the space inside. There is hardly a single straight line there. It is carefully orchestrated between curves and straight lines. The inside was always very important for me and for almost everybody else. I think that is a success of the building: it is incredibly spacious. People are totally shocked when they go inside, and I think pleasantly. It's also the quality of the interior: the soft lines and surfaces, the acoustics (there are 300 people, and you can still work there), the ceiling and the soft carpet.

MT: So you got to the point where you'd finalised the end shape. Everybody had agreed on it. Then Pendennis started going ahead with making it. I assume you were heavily involved at that stage?

JK: Yes, we went down several times to see the first elements being made at Pendennis. They loved working on it, and it was fascinating to watch them. It was not a building site with navvies walking around – these are highly sophisticated people. It was 20 metres long and three and a half metres wide. Part of it was subcontracted to a very famous company in Holland that deals only with aluminium – they build boats but other things as well. We went there, and we saw them assembling the whole roof of the Media Centre, which was 40 metres long – and they were still working on it. It was amazing to see. It was like something medieval, with people climbing all over and welding another piece or replacing stitches, because they stitch it on first like tailors, and then fill and waterproof the welding.

MT: That was all to do with the process of it being delayed. Basically, if it had been assembled at one point before it actually went to Lord's cricket ground it would have been much easier to do.

JK: Yes, definitely. Next time I would absolutely insist with something like that. I would definitely do it completely somewhere and then transport it. The assembly, the cranes, the skill are absolutely amazing. The pieces were all designed so that you didn't even need a police escort, except for two major elements which did need one – they had to go into London overnight. The rest of the building was designed in 3-metre wide elements, and that is the maximum width of the load you can take on the road. You can go today, tomorrow, right now. You don't need any permission.

MT: Is the majority of it basically prefabricated?

JK: Inside, yes. It's very simple, and it's also unique. That's another thing people didn't understand. We always promised that the same contractor – that's Pendennis – would take care of the interior. They used exactly the same techniques as they use in boats. The hanging of the insulation was a major problem – another breakthrough in this building. It has to be said that without Arups we wouldn't have been able to do it, because they convinced the fire officer and building control that this was possible, that the aluminium would not melt behind this certain type of insulation.

MT: How did the interior colour come about?

JK: Almost by accident, as these things do. One day, on the bus or the train, I suddenly realised. We knew about the lining. I always wanted the lining inside to be soft. That was taken directly from yachts. Then you have a choice of colours. I thought, 'Why not use some colour all the way through?' I did a sketch of the thing from the outside. The first time you see white outside. Then you put a little bit of colour pencil on the glass elevation, and you see it light blue. Blue is notoriously good for avoiding reflection. They always paint the walls and barriers in cricket grounds light blue, because it's the best thing for absorbing the light and not reflecting. The blue makes it more integrated as well – you don't see the dark silhouettes of people against a white background. I wanted to put a little bit of blue on the legs. They rejected that, but it would have made it even lighter and smaller. There was no chance of pushing that, but I don't mind too much.

MT: Did you have to do quite a lot of fighting as far as the financial side of it went?

JK: Oh, yes. All the time. There was even one stage when the building was half empty, and somebody in a long meeting said, 'We can't carry on.' They decided that it would stay as it was – half unfurnished. It was taken seriously for about two weeks. But these are unimportant stories. The important story is how it was done and the brave people around the project.

MT: On the interior, how much say did you have on final finishing?

JK: The main concept came very close very early on from writers. The balcony and the mezzanine for the television and radio were there from day one of the original competition. I thought the restaurant guys should see the game as well. So we didn't lose anything conceptual. We didn't lose the colour – there was a long battle. We lost a couple of hinges, which they replaced. We have increased the loos – that's not a loss. We had endless battles about the fixed furniture, but finally we got almost everything we wanted. The lining is there. The carpet is there, except that the colour was changed because the NatWest people said the blue looked too much like Barclays. I wanted to have some old bats – there are millions of these around – or photographs of the players. But in the main the design is pretty much as we intended – we got about 95 per cent of what we wanted.

MT: At the end of the day, I assume you are proud of the building.

JK: Oh, yes.

MT: Is there anything you would do differently if you had to live it again?

JK: Very few things. The cladding on the legs should be something slightly different … but I wouldn't change the shape. I would refine it, but not much.

MT: You would refine it aesthetically?

JK: Yes. You experience the real object against drawings and computer images. That is experience you can't match. Those who design cars have an advantage; they make a full-size model first. We don't have that possibility. So you can refine the form, and I certainly would improve on the legs, but apart from that I'm quite satisfied – particularly since I've taken around certain important architects, and they have praised it. I also see the future – how to use that, how to push it forward. It's not the technical aspect. I will be very sad if people see it as that. It's only serving a purpose. There is no new technology – there's only technology that's new to the building industry. The MCC wanted to have a building, so we achieved that one way or another. That's how it goes. The technology was a supporting mechanism of the thinking on both sides. People think that this is somehow a technical achievement, but it's actually a human achievement, because those 300 guys inside like it. One thing I would love would be if someone said it was elegant. There are comments about space stations and all this rubbish, but funnily enough, when the camera went on it the first reaction and the first joke were absolutely great, and then there was peace and quiet. It's there, and it's maybe alien and designed by one skirt and one eccentric foreigner. That's fine. If somebody says it's an alien object or a space station, I laugh, because space stations don't look like that at all.

6. Amanda Levete, Partner, Future Systems

AL: The way we got to know the MCC was out of the blue, and it was at a time when we didn't have much work. We got a phone call from Peter Bell who was then a member of the working party of the sites group. They wanted a screen that was invisible from the spectators' side but which you couldn't see through from the players' side. They came to us as a last resort because other people had a look at it, but nobody had solved it. Peter Bell knew of our work; he knew that we had a reputation for being a bit lateral, a bit quirky. It was a real last resort for them.

We went along to the MCC to be briefed. It was the first time that Jan and I went there and of course he wasn't wearing a tie. We were shown into a little ante-room and the steward looked us up and down, because clearly we weren't properly dressed. Anyway, we were briefed, and we came up, with Arups, with what everybody thought was a brilliant solution. We patented it jointly with the MCC, but then some added complications arose about what it needed to do, so for one reason or another it didn't go ahead. But we'd made an impact – we had come up with a solution, and I think they quite liked us although they thought we were a bit mad.

Then, about six months later, Peter mentioned that there would be this media centre, and invited us to join the competition. We had the brief and it just seemed like a golden opportunity, tailor-made for us, absolutely extraordinary that it would be raised above the ground so that everybody could view the boundaries. By that point Tony Lewis had decided on the position as well. The brief was basically to design a state-of-the-art media centre that allowed every writer and every broadcaster to see right to the boundaries – and there had to be no reflections on the pitch. At the time we again had very little work and I was pregnant and we were concerned about the future – so little work in fact, that Jan had already done that seminal sketch with the single support before we got the brief. When we got

the competition brief through, we just went for it. Jan had come up with this idea on site and we just knew it was right. But it was much bigger than we imagined so it needed to be supported on two columns rather than one.

MT: How do you work through the design process? A lot of people seem to see Jan as the designer and you as the practical one. How true is that?

AL: If you want to put people into defined roles, generally yes, Jan is very much the designer, but my interest is in building. If you look at Jan's work before I joined him, building is not what drives him. What drives Jan is drawing, pure creativity. But what drives me is building. It's not just building Jan's dream, it's making Jan's dream better and making it into a vision that is shared by the office. Jan has a very particular way of looking at the world, a very particular 'take' on things, a very particular aesthetic which is extremely powerful and very original, but it does need to be challenged. It's quite difficult to challenge Jan – not everyone's up for it, but I am!

As far as the Media Centre is concerned, we put everything into it – Jan was driving the design a bit, but I was driving the process of it being realised and all the liaison with the MCC – not an easy group of people, and all men. I remember the first time we were in a working party with them and I needed to go to the loo. At that time, they didn't have women members coming into the pavilion. I had to be escorted along this tortuous route upstairs by one of the stewards. We got to the door and it had a sign 'Gents' and he just turned it over and it said 'Ladies' – it was just unreal. After that, I was allowed to go by myself. Anyway, as I said, Jan was the driving force behind the design. When he comes up with an initial sketch, it doesn't always hit bullseye, but on this occasion it did. It was then just a question of developing it, manipulating it until it was better, until it looked really beautiful. But why it felt so right for us as a project was because it was as much about the technical as the artistic – functionality meets instinct. I think that really is what our work is about. You need both; you can't just have one. In the past our reputation has focused on the technical and perhaps that was our fault, it was Jan's way of explaining and justifying things. But in fact it's not — it's very subjective, it's instinctive.

I have to say that maybe one of the measures of the success of the project is that we didn't have to explain it — it has caught people's imagination, touched people, excited people, and we knew when it was right. You know it didn't look particularly elegant at every stage — and it was a question of doing the line, working on it, until it looked right; and we went for broke in the competition stage. We had this discussion about tempering it, but we had the confidence that it was the right thing to do, so we decided to be completely uncompromising.

We knew how it could be constructed by a boat builder, so we put the competition report together, mentioning the boat builders and then presented it. It was very much to do with the kind of technology that Jan in particular has been talking about for more than ten years, so it was a logical development. I remember we were finishing off the competition just at the point when I had Josef, and the two weeks after he was born were a nightmare because I was trying to finish writing the report — my fantasies of working at home with this sleeping baby were blown apart on day one. But we finally finished it, and we had to present it to the working party with Arups and the rest of the design team. Then developing the design was very much a joint effort: some designs are quite painful and there's a lot of friction, but in this one there wasn't because we just felt it was right — it really did flow naturally.

Then we were down to the last two and we were asked to make certain adjustments — us and David Morley. They asked us to re-do the report, to take off the flags from the top — which I thought was a very good idea because they actually spoilt the line — and to take out any references to boat building, which was not such a good idea. We went along with

it, and then finally we won it and we were appointed. It took a long time from April to November or December to win the competition formally, but it was then about realising the effect that this was going to have on us and realising that we couldn't do it from the space we had, that we needed to take more people on, that we needed to have a more grown-up set-up. Jan isn't very good at dealing with change and didn't really like the idea of expanding — although he was excited about it, he was worried about loss of control. Anyway, we moved office and then we moved house and it was just a nightmare — but very exciting. We took two or three people on including David Miller as Project Architect. David came from Calatrava's office and he made an important contribution to the project. We started designing by hand, which was unreal when you think back. It was only the pressure from the people at the office that made us buy computers — 'We're going to leave unless you do' — because neither Jan nor I are computer literate, and that was a big step for the office, a big step for Jan.

MT: Has that changed since?

AL: No, Jan doesn't use a computer — won't have one on his desk, doesn't want to, doesn't have to — so we don't have a computerised diary system, and we still run round with the paper diary. I'm networked into the rest of the office. Jan still feels that computers take away from the creative process; he feels it's a threat that you're not thinking with a pencil, that you're thinking in a different way. And it's true, you do think in a different way, but it transformed the office, it made it possible. We wouldn't have got it done without.

MT: But the drawings were still being done by hand?

AL: The conceptual drawings were still being done by hand, the manipulation of the form was done by hand and even a lot of the form-finding process was done by hand, ironically. We did it the long way round — it was a big learning curve for us, but you can't produce information now like that. So that was very exciting. It was a ground-breaking project – technically and aesthetically. It was functionally very complex, out of all proportion to the size and the value of the project. There were the IT requirements, and there were the visual requirements: not having reflections on the ground; batsmen not being able to see themselves in the glass; the fact that it was facing due west but we couldn't have the kind of shading that you might have had on a conventional building because then you would obliterate the views for some of the people. You were trying to get an enormous number of people into as compact a space as possible and there was a requirement for a restaurant and bar and two hospitality suites on each end. And then throughout the whole process budget was a very keen thing.

I think the initial budget was probably an underestimate, over-optimistic, given the ambition of the project. It's much more than just creating a media centre; it's about repositioning – it's stuffed with the world's media, and it is very highly scrutinised … and it was a very long and difficult process.

MT: What was the biggest area of the budget?

AL: It was the shell, but there were a lot of reasons for that. The MCC did get very nervous: I think when they took it on, they didn't realise the enormity of the difference between this building and all the others – I don't think any of us did. We battled very hard to persuade them to use the boat builders. If we'd lost that we would have lost the whole thing. And we would have lost a lot of design control if we hadn't won all these battles, but fortunately we did win most of them. We made life very difficult for ourselves by constantly battling for what we thought was the best. It was a stimulating but very draining time.

MT: Because they were trying to persuade you to go for a more conventional building method?

AL: No, it wasn't that – but they were always trying to reduce

risk as they perceived it and so take control away from the design team and give it to a contractor who they thought could have done it – a contractor like Bovis or McAlpine, but of course they ran a mile because it was using technology that is not common to them. Henk was fantastic. The way that the building got finished was all about relationships and we did strike up a very good relationship with Henk right from the beginning. If we hadn't had that, we wouldn't have been able to persuade him to hang on in there at the times of uncertainty in the project – because he was on the point of backing out on a couple of occasions. Because of the complexity of the job, because we were breaking such new ground, he lost a lot of money; we lost a phenomenal amount of money – it nearly finished us. Also, because we were so focused on that job, we didn't think about what would happen after it. We were running such a tight ship financially and with such a highly controlled team, we just didn't look outside the project. But these are just stories, and now it's paying off.

People say, 'Would you do it again?' and the thing is, for all the tears, we probably would. We learned a lot and it gave us confidence. If we can realise a job like that, a project as complicated as that, and deal with a client as large and as strong as the MCC, then we feel we have the confidence to deal with most things.

MT: Were there people in the MCC who objected to the design?

AL: No. When they put it to their membership, 80 percent voted in favour, which was absolutely extraordinary, given their conservativism. I remember the moment when we put the application in for planning permission. Normally we would talk to the planners right at the beginning to take them along with our way of thinking and set out our objectives; but the MCC had their own planning consultant, Gerald Eve, who had done all the work at Lord's and wanted to do it in a different way, which was to develop the design to a very detailed level and then put it in … so it was very much take it or leave it.

I was nervous about that approach because it wasn't one that I had used before. I remember going to the planning presentation – it wasn't really a discussion, it was a pure presentation to Michael Lowndes, who was the head of planning at Westminster. When I walked in he said, 'Oh, I know you, you did a very nice house in Islington.' That was a very good start, and then I made the presentation. It was very informal – I sat down and he said, 'I think this is a brilliant design. You have my full support. I admire the MCC for being such an enlightened client, for being patrons. I think this work is wonderful and we will do whatever we can do to support you.'

It was so great, so refreshing. The same thing happened when we presented it to the Royal Fine Arts Commission. When we made a presentation to English Heritage, they weren't immediately responsive, but I think it was partly because of the particular officer who was there, who was quite junior. When it went higher up, they were very supportive and put it in their annual report as an example of excellence in design. It's one of those things you can't really explain – I believe that when something's right, when it communicates directly, then people will accept it however radical it is. And that is what we really strive for – that kind of rightness.

MT: That was not the biggest thing, then – getting it through planning.

AL: That was the easiest bit – it was building it and persuading the MCC to go for boat builders and keeping control that were the biggest challenges.

MT: In what way did you achieve control throughout the process?

AL: There were moments when I felt we would really lose it. The design was never really tinkered with – you couldn't really say, 'Let's make it a bit squarer here' and the MCC was very good in that way. They didn't try to alter the fundamental conceptual thinking and they didn't tinker too much with the

small parts of the design. It was to do with risk – and it was a risky project. I have an enormous admiration for them for taking us on; we had never done anything of that size before. They took us on at face value, and they never asked us to join up with anyone else – we would have refused that anyway. It was fantastic.

There are two people who have been most important – Henk and Peter Bell. Peter has been so important in making Lord's what it is now: he was the one who pushed for Hopkins, he was the one who introduced Nick Grimshaw and David Morley, and it's a real shame that he's no longer on the committee.

There was an independent risk assessment that the MCC commissioned and ironically they never published it and never shared it with us, which was really a shame because we would all have learnt a lot. I know that Henk's view is that Arups were over-cautious. If we were to do it all again, we would start off at a different level of understanding of each other's realms and we might be able to make a more efficient structure. But the cost thing – that building really isn't expensive for what it is. I have shown a lot of people round who are amazed at what we have achieved, and these are people – very hard-bitten developers – who know what things are worth and how much things cost. The cost, like in many building projects, was controlled. The budget was increased at various stages of the job, so it's wrong to say that the competition brief said £2.75 but it ended up costing £5 million without understanding why.

The competition brief was much smaller; it didn't have any air conditioning, it didn't have IT, it didn't have whole loads of other things, so there was a lot that was just development of the brief and the building got bigger and became a lot more sophisticated as the design went along. Also it was to do with the price of aluminium going up and the orders not being placed in time because people were trying to keep options open. We wasted a lot of time looking for alternative procurement routes, maybe four months, maybe more.

MT: Since it's been finished, what's happened to the practice? You said you hadn't really thought about future work.

AL: We finished this in April 1999, and from then until November 1999 we felt as though we were going downhill because we had no new work, even though we were making a really concerted effort to get it. We had a full team of six people – David and Matthew we had taken on to do the project, Angus was already with us and Rachel we took on to do a competition – and we didn't really have the work to sustain them. A lot of people would have made them redundant, but I was very committed to that team – they had been incredibly loyal, we worked very well together, and it felt a bit like a family. It went on for a long time, and we started really getting worried. I thought if we were going to collapse, we might as well all collapse together, and if something does come in, then we will have the people to do it. Other people were saying we'd just got to be tough, that's what it's all about – contraction and expansion – but I kept thinking there must be something just round the corner. I couldn't understand why, having achieved what we had achieved, people weren't asking us to do things like it.

And then, out of the blue, we got a call from Vittorio Radici of Selfridges, who had seen the building from the top of a bus, and was asking if he could come and see us about a project. I didn't think anything of it, but then he came to the office with Martin Illingworth, who is the chief architect at Selfridges, and we all got on well. We showed him our work and he explained this project in Birmingham, which sounded fantastic. I think they were a bit surprised that we were as small as we were, and at the end Vittorio said, 'Well, if this doesn't work out, we are continually renewing things at Selfridges – shop fits …' I thought, 'Oh, here we go.' Just as he left, I said our dream would be to do a department store and he said, yes, that would be his dream too. And then we offered to take him and some of his directors around Lord's,

which we did. We were asked to take part in a week-long competition – we weren't paid to do it, but it was only a week – and we had to produce two A1 boards explaining our approach. We all decided not to design, but just to describe our approach, and Angus and Jan and I worked very hard for a week just putting together two boards. Then the three of us went along and each agreed to cover a different aspect of it.

We made the presentation, and felt it had gone well, because it was very informal. The next day we got a phone call from Vittorio and he said something that wasn't entirely clear, like 'I think we need to go forward on this;' I said, 'Do you mean that we've got the job?' He said 'yes' – what a fantastic moment. About four weeks after that, we got the Stirling Prize and then felt we were on our way.

MT: How do things stand now?

AL: Now, as of next week, we'll be 18 people. It's wonderful, and I hope it will give people a feeling of confidence that we can do big work, because I know we can – and we are: we're doing this huge Selfridges project in Birmingham. It's 250,000 square feet; it's a £60 million project. It's wonderful and it's going really well and what is very refreshing about working Selfridges is that, although it's a PLC, we're working directly with Vittorio. He has a very good team, but he is the one who makes the decisions and he's very courageous and very instinctive and confident. And it's a very creative relationship. We go on site at the end of this year. We're being considered for lots of other things – big things and little things. We're doing some shops for Marni – small but really interesting, again working with the designer.

MT: Would you like to do some more housing projects?

AL: Not unless it's really, really special. Doing houses for people is one of the most difficult and draining things you can do – difficult because you are dealing in a very small scale, so you don't get the same level of support, and draining in that the relationship with the client is always very emotional, very intense. It's their money. I always feel deeply guilty when things come in more expensive, even when we're dealing with people like the MCC. When we choose to do a house, we have to feel that there's some connection between us and the client, because you can't do a house for someone unless you really like each other. The two houses we've done for Jeremy and Debra and Bob and Gill – Jeremy King and Debra Hauer we knew a little bit before we started and we became good friends, Bob and Gill we didn't know at all and became good friends. It's not always easy, but they are very special people. It would be a nightmare otherwise. I do feel we have been very privileged to work with such great clients.

MT: Is there anything else you would like to say about Lord's?

AL: It was a great opportunity … Thank you, MCC!

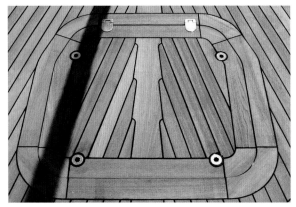

PHOTO P. BELL

PHOTO P. MACKINUEN

PHOTO P. MACKINUEN

PHOTO© JASON HAWKES

PHOTO© AEROFILMS

NOVEMBER 1996

FEBRUARY 1997

OCTOBER 1997

FEBRUARY 1998

FEBRUARY 1998

APRIL 1998

MARCH 1998

APRIL 1998

MARCH 1998

APRIL 1998

APRIL 1998

MAY 1998

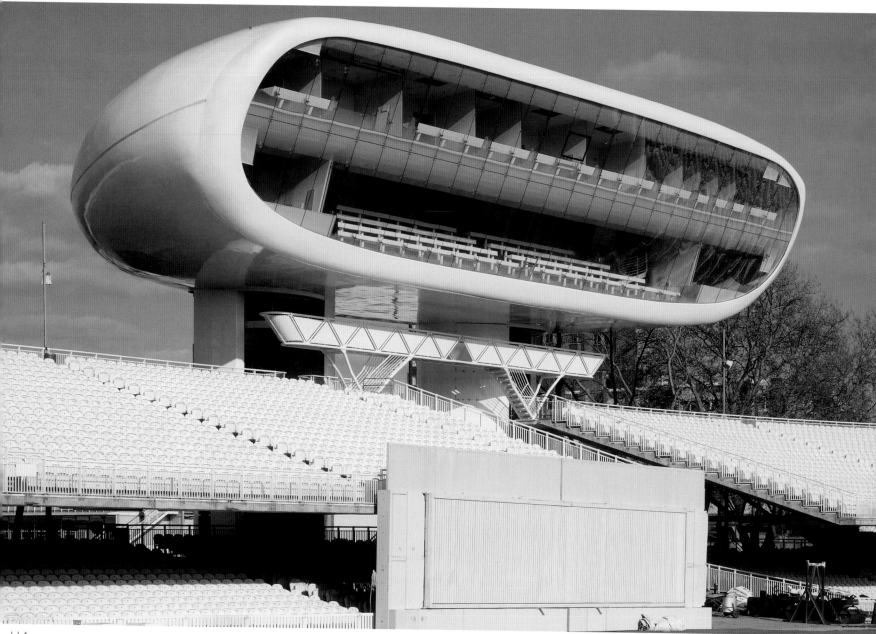

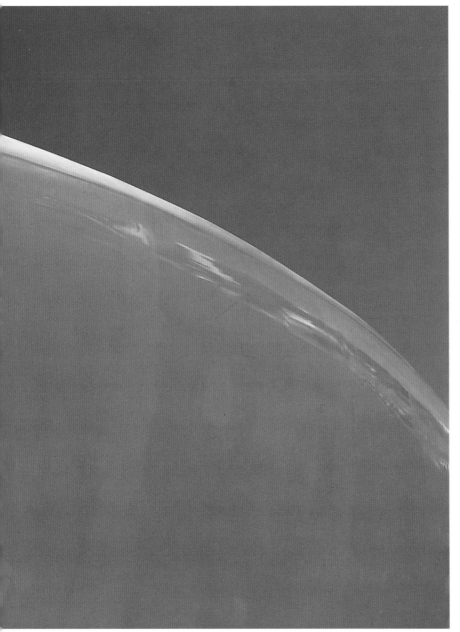

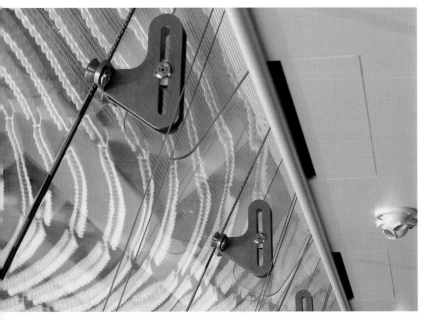

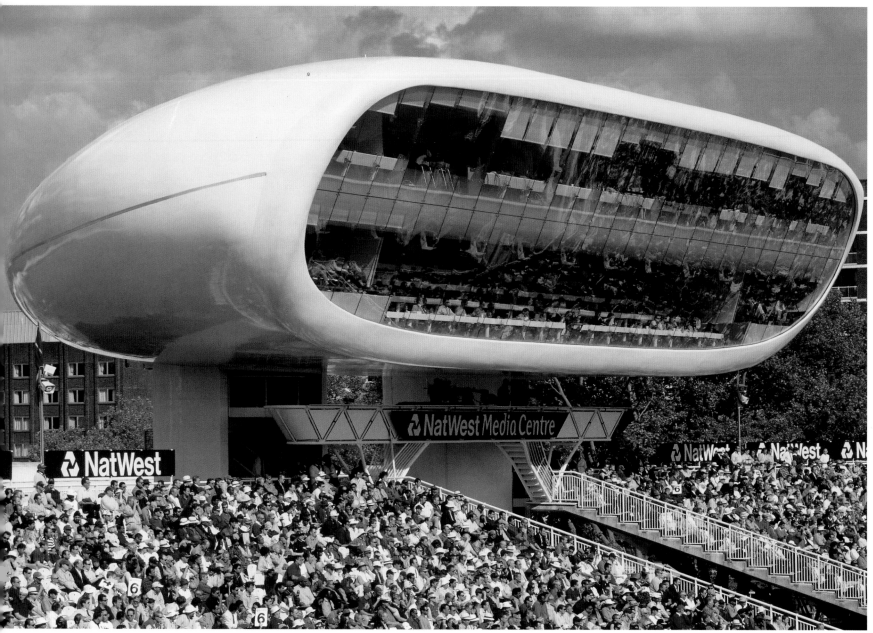

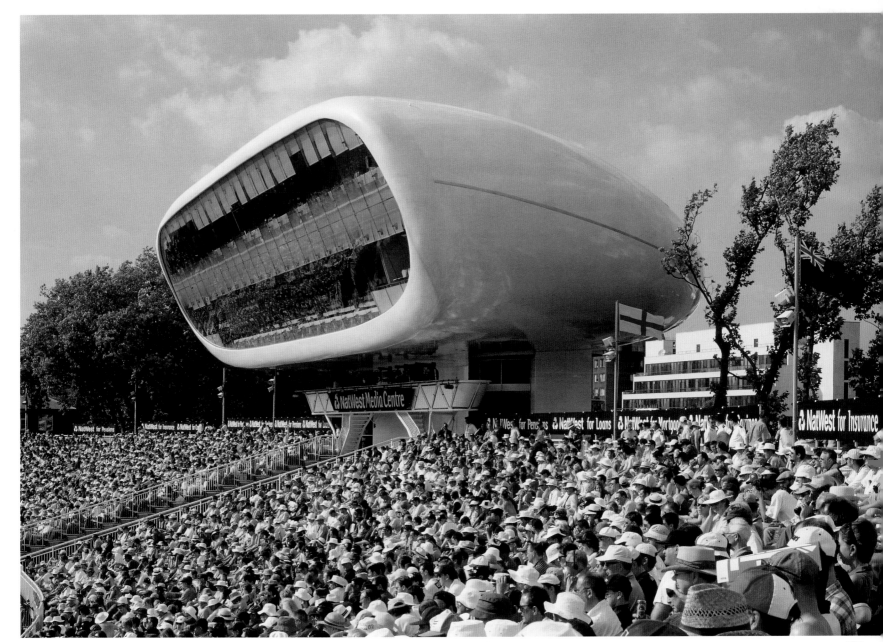

WORLD CUP 1999

WORLD CUP 1999

WORLD CUP 1999

WORLD CUP 1999

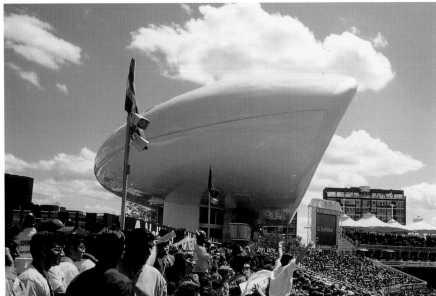

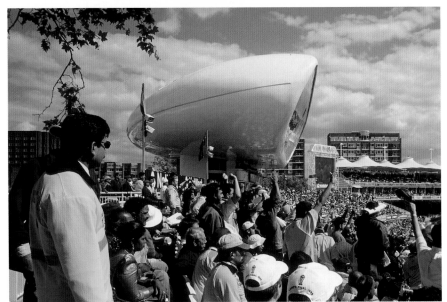

WORLD CUP 1999

Cricket's eye in the sky

DAILY TELEGRAPH

LOOK AT THEIR PRIMITIVE BUILDINGS, CLEARLY SOME SORT OF TEMPLE... YES, I WAS SPOT ON, ITS...

Bug-eyed Lord's press centre wins top design prizes

INDEPENDENT

The Future is here – Media Centre wins Stirling Prize

ARCHITECT'S JOURNAL

Lord's spaceship has landed

THE TIMES

Lord's landmark in line for top award

SUNDAY TELEGRAPH

Better by design
New looks for London and Glasgow
Pages T16 – 17

Wicket peeper

BUILDING SERVICES JOURNAL

The rise of the pod squad

SUNDAY TIMES

Beam me up, Aggers

EVENING STANDARD

Spaceship takes off at Lord's

INDEPENDENT

Lord's invest in alien art

DAILY TELEGRAPH

Basically, it's a garden shed

THE GUARDIAN

Lord's reveals the nautical eye in the sky

DAILY TELEGRAPH

Open wide, the Lord's lozenge has arrived

THE TIMES SATURDAY

Lord's enters the space age

METRO

SPECIFICATIONS

DIMENSIONS: 40m × 20m × 21m

FLOOR AREA: 600m^2

WEIGHT: Superstructure — 90 T

CAPACITY: TV and RADIO   100 Person
WRITERS   120 Person

RESTAURANT: 50 person

STRUCTURE: Aluminium semi-monocoque structure from 32 elements 20m × 3.6m Weight 3–6 T

MATERIALS: Aluminium 5038 Grade Sheet 6–12 mm

TOWERS: Concrete structure with GRP cladding

LIFTS: 2 × 8 Person Lifts

TOTAL COST: £5,000,000

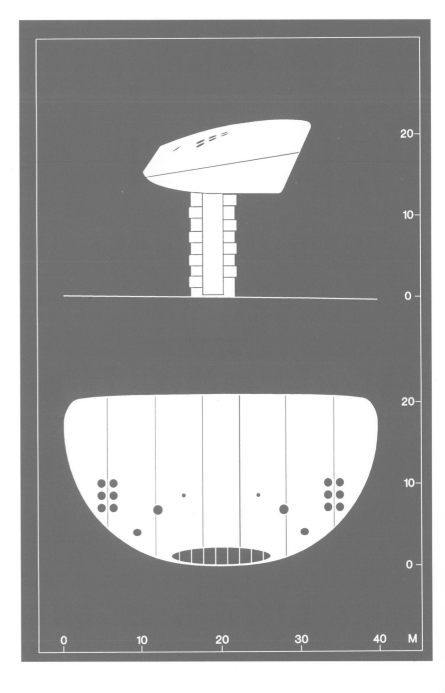

ELEMENTS

MAIN CONTRACTOR: *PENDENNIS SHIPYARD*

Henk Wiekens   David Bentley   Keith Parkin   Andrew Snapes

MANAGEMENT CONTRACTOR – TOWERS: *HEERY INTERNATIONAL*

SUBCONTRACTORS and SUPPLIERS:

Glazing	MAG
Fitted furniture	Wattson Shopfitters
Lighting	Concord Sylvania
Towers, stairs and gantry	Littlehampton Welding
Carpets	Vorwerk Carpets
Mechanical Services	P & D Heating
Electrical Services	Carey Electrical
Rubber Flooring	Dalsouple Direct
Concrete	Geoffrey Osborne
Mobile Bar	The Splinter Group
Ironmongery	Allgoods
Blinds	Levolux
Lifts	Stannah Lifts
IT	GPW
Signage	Cartilage Levene
Catering	Sett Design

TEAM

ARCHITECTS: *FUTURE SYSTEMS*
    Matthew Heywood
    Jan Kaplicky
    Amanda Levete
    David Miller
    Simon Mitchell
    Angus Pond
    Rachel Stevenson

COMPUTER IMAGES: *HAYES DAVIDSON*
    Alan Davidson

COST CONSULTANTS: *DAVIS LANGDON and EVEREST*
    Richard Baldwin
    Roger Barbrook
    Andy Hewitt

FIRE ENGINEERING: *ARUPS FIRE ENGINEERING*
    John Hopkinson

GLAZING CONSULTANT: *BILLINGS DESIGN ASSOCIATES*
    Sean Billings

MODELS: *UNIT 22*
    Don Shuttleworth

SERVICES: *BURO HAPPOLD*
    Neil Billet
    Denzil Gallagher
    Ken Carmichael

STRUCTURE: *OVE ARUP and PARTNERS*
    Anna Broomfield
    Sarah Kaethner
    Ned Stork
    David Glover
    Chris Murgatroyd
    Ian Feltham
    Pat Dallard
    Jonathan Kelly
    Jon McCarthy
    Sara McCreery
    Paula Welsh

SPECIAL CONSULTANT: *P. Bell*

PHOTOGRAPHERS:
    Richard Davies   All photographs except
    Peter Mackinuen   p98, p99
    Nick Kane   p117
    Peter Bell   p94
    Jason Hawkes   p106
    Aerofilms   p13, p107
    Future Systems   p102, p104

CLIENT: *Marylebone Cricket Club*

DIARY

1995
FEBRUARY   First sketch for Marylebone Cricket Club
MAY   Competition of four Teams
OCTOBER   Competition of two Teams
NOVEMBER   Marylebone Cricket Club announces the winners – FUTURE SYSTEMS

1996
APRIL   Preliminary Tender from Pendennis Shipyard
JUNE   Marylebone Cricket Club Press Conference
JULY   Planning submission
AUGUST   Major Future Systems Presentation to Marylebone Cricket Club
NOVEMBER   Planning permission granted by Westminster City Council
DECEMBER   Site work started – Towers

1997
FEBRUARY   Construction of first construction unit started at Pendennis Shipyard
APRIL   Future Systems Production drawings completed
MAY   Towers foundations completed
NOVEMBER   Towers superstructure completed
DECEMBER   First structural unit arrives at Lord's Cricket Ground

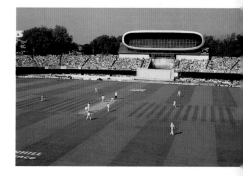

1998
APRIL   Last structural unit arrives at Lord's
MAY   Interiors construction started
APRIL –
SEPTEMBER   Cricket season in progress – Interiors construction continues

1999
FEBRUARY   Interiors construction completed
APRIL   Marylebone Cricket Club Press Conferences and opening ceremony lunch
JUNE   Media Centre completed – First Match
JULY   World Cup – Building used by 250 journalists
DECEMBER   Stirling Prize awarded to Future Systems for the Media Centre Building

AWARDS

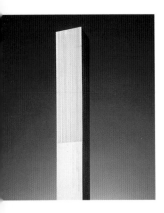

Aluminium Imagination Architectural Award – Main Prize

1999 British Institute of Architectural Technology – Major Commendation

Millennium Products – For Creative and Innovative Products

1999 British Construction Industry – Building Award

RIBA The Stirling Prize for Architecture – RIBA Building of the Year

RIBA Category Awards Architecture in Arts and Leisure Award

Institute of Structural Engineers – Structural Achievement Award

ICE London Merit Award 2000

ALUMINIUM IMAGINATION
THE 1999 AWARDS DINNER

at The Ballroom
The Dorchester Hotel
Park Lane, London W1
10 June 1999

7.15 pm Reception
8.00 pm Dinner
Black Tie

Ballroom Entrance
Admission by ticket only

MAIN SPONSOR
THE ALUMINIUM EXTRUDERS ASSOCIATION
SUPPORTED BY THE INDEPENDENT

ADDITIONAL SPONSORSHIP RECEIVED FROM THE ALUMINIUM ROLLED PRODUCTS
MANUFACTURERS ASSOCIATION (ARPMA), THE COUNCIL FOR ALUMINIUM IN BUILDING (CAB),
THE ALUMINIUM FINISHING ASSOCIATION (AFA) AND THE ARCHITECTS' JOURNAL.